# The Business Writing
# Style Book

# THE BUSINESS WRITING STYLE BOOK

John S. Fielden
Jean D. Fielden
Ronald E. Dulek

Prentice-Hall, Inc., Englewood Cliffs, New Jersey

Prentice-Hall International, Inc., *London*
Prentice-Hall of Australia, Pty. Ltd., *Sydney*
Prentice-Hall Canada, Inc., *Toronto*
Prentice-Hall of India Private Ltd., *New Delhi*
Prentice-Hall of Japan, Inc., *Tokyo*
Prentice-Hall of Southeast Asia Pte. Ltd., *Singapore*
Whitehall Books, Ltd., Wellington, *New Zealand*
Editora Prentice-Hall do Brasil Ltda., *Rio de Janeiro*

© 1984 by

PRENTICE-HALL, INC.

Englewood Cliffs, N.J.

**Library of Congress Cataloging in Publication Data**

Fielden, John S.
  The business writing style book.

  Includes index.
  1. English language—Business English.   2. Persuasion
(Rhetoric)   3. English language—Self-instruction.
I. Fielden, Jean D.   II. Dulek, Ronald E.   III. Title.
PE1479.B87F53 1984    808'.066651    83-19208
ISBN 0-13-108290-6

Printed in the United States of America

# THE AUTHORS

*John S. Fielden, Ph.D.,* University Professor of Management Communications, University of Alabama, is the author of nine *Harvard Business Review* articles, including the all-time *Harvard Business Review* classic, "What Do You Mean I Can't Write?" A consultant to IBM since 1964, Dr. Fielden is formerly Dean of the Business Schools of Boston University and the University of Alabama. He is a writing consultant to General Electric, Dun and Bradstreet, General Foods and other U.S. and Canadian firms.

*Jean D. Fielden, Ph.D.,* Board of Visitors Research Professor and Chairman of the Applied Statistics Program at the University of Alabama, was formerly an Associate Professor at The Wharton School of Finance and Commerce. She is a Fellow of the American Statistical Association and the International Statistical Association. Her major authorships include four books and numerous articles on quantitative tests for decision making.

*Ronald E. Dulek, Ph.D.,* is Associate Professor and Coordinator of Management Communications at the University of Alabama. He is consultant to IBM, OSHA, the United States Department of Health and Human Services, AT&T, and other public and private organizations. His articles on business communications have been published in *Business Horizons, Journal of Business Communications, Personnel Journal, Personnel* magazine, and *IEEE Transactions on Professional Communications.*

## ACKNOWLEDGMENTS

We wish to acknowledge the valuable contributions made to the development of materials in this book by Cal Knickerbocker and Lamar Bordelon of the National Accounts Division of IBM.

# A MESSAGE ABOUT THIS UNIQUE BOOK

We first became aware that there were style wars going on when we were doing some consulting on management communications for a very large corporation. Here we found people playing a sort of paddleball, using drafts of letters instead of balls. Volley after volley went back and forth between those who signed letters and those who actually wrote them. It was a game nobody liked, but it continued, and the company paid dearly.

What caused this round-robin of revision? Typos? Factual misstatements? Poor format? No. *Style* did.

Is your company conducting a style war? Ask yourself how often you hear statements like these:

> It takes a new assistant about a year to learn my style. Until he does, I have no choice but to bounce letters back for revision. I won't sign a letter if it doesn't sound like me.

> I find it difficult, almost impossible, to write letters for my boss's signature. His style is different from mine.

Soon, however, we discovered that style problems did not plague just large organizations. In smaller organizations, where people usually wrote and signed their own letters, confusion about style also reigned. A letter goes out. The reaction from the reader is not at all what the writer desired. It gets reported back that the reader didn't like the writer's style. A colleague looks over a copy of the letter and says, "No wonder the reader didn't like your letter. You shouldn't have said things the way you did. Your style is all wrong."

"Style? What's wrong with my style?"

"I don't know," comes the response. "I just don't like the way you said things."

The cost of this guessing game about what style is effective may be staggering, especially if your company's work requires much writing. A Xerox study indicated that professional personnel in industries such as information handling, communications, banking, insurance, education, consulting, government, broadcasting, and publishing spend 52 percent of their time reading and writing; their managers spend 56 percent.*

How much of this reading and writing time is wasted in playing the foolish letter paddleball game of seemingly endless rejection and revision? Our impression is that it is a very sizeable percentage. And for companies across the United States, this waste must add up to billions of dollars.

But let's not dwell on such speculation. There is little you can do as an individual to cure such a widespread business problem. What you *can* do is ask yourself this:

> How can I become more productive in performing my writing tasks? How can I learn to write letters and memos that are close to the mark on the first attempt? In short, how can I learn to know what I'm doing when I write?

*The Business Writing Style Book*, we believe, will set you on the right track to being more personally productive and more successful in your business writing. And if enough individuals are helped, possibly this will help solve the broader national problem.

---

*Reported in "The Management Workstation," International Data Corporation, May 1981, p. 21.

## ORIGIN OF THIS BOOK

In researching some communications problems experienced by one of the nation's largest and best-managed companies, we found to our astonishment that:

- One of this corporation's division headquarters alone mailed 9 million communications annually!
- Between 5 and 10 percent of those 9 million communications were letters, memos, and reports written to persons inside and outside the corporation. (The rest of the communications were brochures, announcements, policy statements, product descriptions, and the like, often sent out by the thousands.)
- If we take the 5 percent figure, we have 450,000 individually signed messages sent annually by this one divisional headquarters.
- Of those 450,000 letters and memos, 15 percent were signed by the writer; 85 percent were written for another's signature.
- Of those written for another's signature, 85 percent were rejected for revision by the signer.
- Of those rejected, almost all were turned down because of stylistic objections (the signer didn't like the way something was said).

Simple arithmetic shows that 85 percent of 450,000 amounts to 382,000 letters and memos written for another's signature. And if 85 percent of those are rejected for revision, then the total of rejected messages equals 325,125.

In the opinion of managers interviewed, the average number of revisions these 325,125 rejected memos and letters received was five! Therefore, 5 times 325,125 equals 1,625,625 revised drafts.

Estimate for yourself the cost of each draft. Five dollars seems an extremely modest estimate; ten dollars is more likely. But even if we settle for five dollars, here's what results:

1,625,625 times $5 equals more than $8,128,125 per year!

And this was for only one division of that well-managed company! More than $8 million (and more likely $16 million if ten dollars a revision is used) is sacrificed annually on the altar of writing style, because each signoff level didn't like the way something was said. It's unbelievable, yet true.

That company asked us to offer its people some advice about business writing style. At first, we felt that we couldn't because style is such a vague subject. We didn't know what the word style meant in the business context.

Everybody talks about style, but almost nobody understands the meaning of the word in the business environment. And this lack of understanding hurts both those who write letters for another's signature and those who write for themselves. Neither knows any place to turn for help.

Strunk and White's *The Elements of Style*,* while a marvelous book, spends only fifteen pages on "An Approach to Style," and is not specifically oriented to style in business writing. Many large publishing companies, many learned journals, and some university publishers (Chicago, for instance) have published what they call "Style Manuals" to be followed by authors. These manuals set standards for things such as rules to follow in punctuation; documentation rules for footnoting, making bibliographies, and glossaries; rules for headings and subheadings. Obviously, such style manuals illustrate an entirely different meaning of the word style from that used by business people.

So little has been written about style as it should be defined in business writing that we have had to rely on imagination tempered by practical experience. There was, alas, no other book on business writing style for us to "examine" and "improve upon." Therefore, we were forced to be original. But, let's face it; when one is being truly original, there is always the chance that what one writes will be arrant nonsense. At first we feared that this might be the case.

Therefore, we conducted some experiments. And, then, as you will see, some educated guesses were made about various styles and their impact on the reader. Then these guesses were tested against the reactions of businesspeople. The findings were written up and submitted to the scrutiny of the editors of the *Harvard Business Review.* They liked what was submitted and asked to publish it.* With this independent acceptance of our

---

*William Strunk, Jr., and E. B. White, *The Elements of Style,* MacMillan, 1970.

*Portions of this book reflect ideas developed in John S. Fielden's *Harvard Business Review* article, "What Do You Mean You Don't Like My Style?" (May –June 1982). Copyright © 1982, by the President and Fellows of Harvard College. All rights reserved.

ideas, we became assured that *The Business Writing Style Book* contains information of utility and value to practical business people.

*John S. Fielden*
*Jean D. Fielden*
*Ronald E. Dulek*

---

We have made every effort to avoid sexist language in this text. In situations where a designation is necessary such as in various scenarios, we have alternated with male and female names.

# CONTENTS

# The Business Writing Style Book

# 1

---

## STYLE IS HOW SOMETHING IS SAID—AND SUCCESSFUL WRITING RESULTS FROM SAYING THINGS RIGHT

While everybody talks about style in writing, almost nobody understands the meaning of the word in the business environment. Dictionary and encyclopedia definitions are usually too literary to be useful. They talk about Faulkner's style versus Hemingway's, Shakespeare's style versus Milton's, but there is nothing specifically about business writing styles. Of all the definitions, the following comes closest to defining how businesspeople use the word:

> *Style.* The way something is said or done, as distinguished from its substance.*

This definition makes sense. But is it sufficient for business writing purposes? Managers signing drafts written by subordi-

---

*\*The American Heritage Dictionary of the English Language,* American Heritage Publishing Company and Houghton-Mifflin Company, 1969.

nates—and the subordinates themselves—already know that the main bone of contention between them is the way things should be said. But what is meant by *way*? In fact, *is* there a way? In trying to find that single way, both managers and subordinates may be chasing a will-o'-the-wisp. There may be no magical way, no perfect universal way of writing things that will fend off criticism of style. There may be no one style of writing in business that is appropriate 1) in all situations, or 2) for all readers—even though managers and subordinates usually talk and behave as if there were.

If style is the way we say things, then writing style results from the particular words we select to express our ideas and the types of sentences and paragraphs we employ to deliver those ideas. What else can writing style result from? In writing, there is no tone of voice or body gesture to impart additional meaning. In written business communication, as we will see later, tone comes from what a reader reads into the words and sentences used. Style is in the writing; tone is how the reader emotionally reacts to the writing.

## PURPOSE IS THE KEY

What is the main difference between literary writing and business writing? The answer lies in its purpose. Businesspeople mainly write to a particular person, in a particular situation, to accomplish a particular purpose. Literary artists use a unique style to express themselves to a general audience. Novelists are not writing to accomplish a particular transaction or to get a job done.

If some readers don't like a novelist's way of saying things, nothing much can directly happen to the writer, short of losing some book sales. In the business situation, by contrast, an offensive style may cost the writer a customer, a sale, a promotion, or even a job.

Therefore, effective style in business writing, while it can be distinguished from substance, cannot be divorced from substance—nor from the circumstances under which something is written—nor from the likes, dislikes, position, and power of the reader. Hence, a workable definition of style in business writing is this:

*Style:* That choice of words, sentences, and paragraphing, which, by virtue of being appropriate to the message situation and to the relative power position of writer and reader, will produce the desired reaction end result.

# KEYS TO DETERMINING YOUR STYLE

Let's see what we can learn from a case situation. Assume that you are an executive in a very large information processing company. You receive the following letter.

Community General Hospital
Anytown, U.S.A.

Ms./Mr. _____
XYZ Corporation
Anytown, U.S.A. 12345

Dear _____,

As you know, I respect your professional opinion highly. The advice your people have given us at ABCD Corporation, as we have moved into a comprehensive information system over the past three years, has been very helpful.

I'm writing to you now, however, in my role as Chairman of the Executive Committee of the Trustees of our hospital. We at Community General Hospital have decided to establish a skilled (volunteer) data processing evaluation team to assess proposals to automate our hospital's information flow.

I have suggested your name to my committee as a member of that evaluation team. I know you can get real satisfaction by helping your community in this way. Please say yes. I look forward to being able to count on your advice. Let me hear from you soon.

Frank J. Scalpel
Chairman, Executive Committee

As an executive with XYZ, Inc., you would be in a conflict of interest situation if you accepted this appointment. You know that XYZ will be submitting a proposal to install a comprehensive information system for Community General Hospital. However, Mr. Scalpel is the vice-president of finance of ABCD Corporation, a very good customer of your company. You know Scalpel well, having worked with him on community programs as well as in the business situation.

Read the following four draft versions of a letter to Mr. Scalpel. Each version says essentially the same thing, but each is written in a different (but typical) business style. These are, of course, not the only possible styles in which a letter could be drafted, but they are typical and lend themselves to profitable discussion. As you read each version, think about its style and answer these questions:

Does the style seem:
    Forceful or passive?
    Personal or impersonal?
    Colorful or colorless?

Then answer these questions:

| Of the various versions: | I | II | III | IV |
|---|---|---|---|---|
| Which one's style do you like best? | ___ | ___ | ___ | ___ |
| Which one's style most resembles the style you customarily use? | ___ | ___ | ___ | ___ |

*Version I*

Dear Mr. Scalpel,

    As you realize, this litigious age makes it necessary for large companies often to take stringent measures not only to avoid conflicts of interest on the part of their employees, but also to preclude even the very suggestion of conflict. And, since my company intends to submit a proposal with reference to automating the hospital's information flow, it would not appear seemly for me to be part of an evaluation team assessing competitors' proposals. Even if I were to excuse myself from consideration of the XYZ proposal, I still would be vulnerable to charges that I gave short shrift to competitors' offerings.

If there is any other way that I can serve the committee that will not raise this conflict of interest specter, you know that I would find it pleasurable to be of service as always.

Sincerely,

### Version II

Dear Frank,

Your comments relative to your respect for my professional opinion are most appreciated. Moreover, your invitation to serve on the hospital's data processing evaluation team is received with gratitude, albeit with some concern.

The evaluation team must be composed of persons free of alliances with any of the vendors submitting proposals. For that reason, it is felt that my services on the team could be construed as a conflict of interest.

Perhaps help can be given in some other way. Again, please be assured that your invitation has been appreciated.

Sincerely,

### Version III

Dear Frank,

Thanks for suggesting my name as a possible member of your data processing evaluation team. I wish I could serve, but I cannot.

XYZ intends, naturally, to submit a proposal to automate the hospital's information flow. You can see the position of conflict I would be in if I were on the evaluation team.

Just let me know of any other way I can be of help. You know I would be more than willing. Thanks again for the invitation.

*Version IV*

Dear Frank,

Thanks for the kind words and the invitation. Sure wish I could say yes. Can't, though.

XYZ intends to submit a sure-fire proposal on automating the hospital's information. Shouldn't be a judge and advocate at the same time!

Any other way I can help ... just give me a buzz. Thanks again.

Cordially,

## LET'S COMPARE REACTIONS

Now that you've given your reactions, jotted down your stylistic preferences, and explored at least superficially the emotional reactions underlying your preferences, compare your notes with the following observations.

Version I is cold, impersonal, complex. Most people react somewhat negatively to this style of prose because it seems to push them away from the writer. It reveals through word choice a cerebral quality on the part of the writer that, while flattering the reader's intelligence, also seems to parade that of the writer. Most businesspeople would not like this style.

Version II will score fairly cool, quite impersonal. Readers' reactions will probably be neither strongly positive nor strongly negative. This style of writing is essentially "blah." The reason is that it is heavily passive. Instead of saying, "I appreciate your comments," it says, "Your comments are most appreciated," "Your invitation is received," "It is felt that my services could be construed...." This use of the passive voice enables the writer to be subordinated modestly to the back of sentences or to disappear completely. (I appreciated your comments. Your comments were appreciated by me. Your comments were appreciated.)

This is the impersonal style of writing that many persons with engineering, mathematics, or scientific backgrounds will find most congenial. It is harmless, but it is certainly not colorful, nor is it forceful or interesting. Yet many persons will recognize it as their own style.

Version III is the style of writing that most very high-level executives tend to use. It is simple; it is personal; it is warm without being syrupy; it is forceful like a firm handshake. Almost everybody in business will like this style, although lower-level managers often find themselves afraid to write so forthrightly (and, as a result, often find themselves retreating into the styles of versions I and II: version I to make themselves look smart to superiors, or version II so as to appear less bossy and less personal). Persons who find version II congenial tend to be a bit dubious about the appropriateness of version III. Although we have no way of proving this judgment, we would guess that more higher-position persons—owners or managers—will like version III than will lower-position persons.

Version IV goes beyond being forceful; it becomes self-confident to the point of being breezy. It is colorful and conversational to an extreme. And it is so intensely personal and warm that many businesspeople would reject it out of hand, even if they were a very close acquaintance of Frank Scalpel's. "Sounds like an advertising person's chit-chat," some will say. "The extremely informal style does not convey to Mr. Scalpel the seriousness with which you took his invitation," others will say. The persons who like this style (and think Mr. Scalpel will also) will say, "It is a warm, personal, simple style—so why shouldn't it have a positive effect on Mr. Scalpel?"

## WHICH STYLES ARE WINNERS AND WHICH ARE LOSERS?—AND WHY?

As you compared your responses to the four versions with ours, didn't you find yourself objecting to most of the questions asked? Weren't you saying, "What difference does it make which version *I* like? Or which most resembles *my* customary style? Or whether the version is colorful or colorless, forceful or passive, personal or impersonal—in the abstract? What matters is which version will go over best with Mr. Scalpel in this situation!" Now we're getting somewhere.

That is why those who may have wanted to add the words, "and that style should sound like me," to our earlier definition of business writing style were wrong. Circumstances not only alter cases; they alter the "you" that it is wise for your style to project.

Sometimes it's wise to be forceful; at other times it would be suicidal. Sometimes being sprightly and colorful is appropriate; at other times it would be ludicrous. There are times to be personal in style and times to be highly impersonal.

That is why the paddleball game between managers and subordinates goes volleying on. The subordinate is trying to imitate the boss's style when in actuality—unless the manager is extremely insensitive—he or she has no universal style for all circumstances and for all readers. Here's what takes place:

1. Subordinates sooner or later get a letter signed. "Aha!" they say, *"That's* the style the boss wants!"
2. Then, they try to use that same style in all situations and with all readers.
3. The bosses begin rejecting drafts written in the very style they formerly professed liking.
4. Both parties throw up their hands.

This is foolish and wasteful. Both parties have to recognize that in business writing style cannot be considered apart from the given situation or from the viewpoint of a single person. Expert writers select the style that fits the situation and the particular reader's needs. Different situations call for different styles.

But having concluded that, do we just walk away? Or is there advice that can be given? We think so. That is what this book is all about. Before we can proceed to select a style strategy to fit the situation, we must classify the various business writing situations that often arise. A rather crude classification that will suit our purposes at present is as follows:

1. *Negative (bad news) situations*—messages saying no or relaying bad news.
2. *Positive (good news) situations*—messages saying yes or conveying good news.
3. *Persuasive (action request) situations*—messages making requests or persuading someone to do something.
4. *Information-conveying situations*—messages that simply relay facts and have little or no possibility of causing any emotional reaction (good or bad) in the reader.

# 3

## DON'T CONFUSE ORGANIZATION WITH STYLE— THEY'RE TWO COMPLETELY DIFFERENT ASPECTS OF SUCCESSFUL WRITING

Every communication has (or should have) some kind of organizational pattern. In this book, we will consider organization as separate from style. Why do we do so? If style is the way something is said, why then is the organizational pattern used to express those thoughts not a part of style?

There are two reasons why we think it logical and wise not to consider organization a part of style:

1. An organizational pattern means the order in which ideas are presented. And order of presentation, by definition, implies a chronology of expression—*when* "this" is said, and *when* "that" is said. But when something is said is not the same as how something is expressed. To introduce chronology into style by making organizational pattern a part of style is to introduce an unnecessarily complicating—and illogical—factor.

2. An understanding of style is difficult enough without throwing everything into the term. Too many style books lump together such wildly disparate elements as grammar, footnoting, and bits of no doubt useful advice such as "Do not use dialect unless your ear is good" (the latter from Strunk and White's style section); this practice has already contributed enough to the businessperson's confusion about this critically important word.

If we pry our working definition open so as to make *when* we say things a part of the *way* we say things, where would we draw the line? Couldn't one argue equally well that punctuation is part of how we say things in writing? And footnotes? And bibliographies?

That way lies, if not madness, at least mass confusion. We need to define business writing style in clear, simple, distinctive terms so that businesspeople can talk sensibly when they discuss writing problems. Therefore (if only because it contributes to simplicity), organizational pattern is defined here as an aspect of writing not included under style.

---

## THE TWO BASIC ORGANIZATIONAL PATTERNS

When all is said and done, there are basically only two organizational patterns that can be used in the four basic types of business messages:

1. *The bottom-line (direct) pattern,* in which the main thrust of the message (its bottom line) is presented as quickly and straightforwardly as possible.
2. *The circuitous (indirect) pattern,* in which the information and purpose of the message are not forthrightly and promptly disclosed, but are held back until the reader's mind has been conditioned and prepared to accept the information.

Which of these two organizational patterns should be used depends on the type of message to be conveyed.

The bottom-line pattern should be used primarily in positive (good news) situations, positive types of persuasive (action request) situations, and information-conveying situations. The primary reason for this recommendation is that we usually have nothing to lose by being direct in each of these positive situations. There is no need to beat around the bush in such communications because the reader's emotional reaction to a positive message is, obviously, positive.

On the other hand, the circuitous pattern is usually used in persuasive messages where someone is being sold something or talked into something. This pattern is also used extensively in negative (bad news) situations and negative types of persuasive (action request) situations. For the latter kinds of messages, there is often a need to bury, delay, or at least soften the negative thrust of the communication, rather than hit the reader immediately over the head with the negative.

For instance, in the case we used in section 2 about Scalpel inviting you to serve on the hospital's evaulation team, you are in a situation of saying no to a very important customer of your company. In fact, you are in a doubly sensitive situation because it is likely that Scalpel does recognize that he is asking you to serve irrespective of your conflict of interest. Therefore, you not only have to tell him no, but you also have to avoid rubbing his nose in the fact that he has actually asked you to do something that is highly unethical. You are faced with communicating two negative messages at once—or else not giving Scalpel any sensible reason for refusing to serve.

This situation, therefore, clearly calls for a circuitous pattern of organization. Let's go back and look again at the four different versions of responses given in section 2.

Version I is very circuitous in organizational pattern. Its rejection of Scalpel is buried appropriately in the middle of the letter.

Version II also is circuitous in pattern. The first paragraph extends some pleasantries and the middle paragraph conveys the negative.

Versions III and IV are both direct in organizational pattern. The rejection occurs in the second sentence of the beginning paragraph of each version.

Hence, in terms of organizational appropriateness to the situation, versions I and II are probably wiser than III and IV. But what about their styles?

# 4

---

# WHICH STYLE CHOICE IS SMART?

So far we have clarified the following terminology for use in our discussions:

- The message is *what* is said.
- Style is the *way* the message is said.
- Organization is *when* (early or late in a communication) or in what order your points will be made.

Now that we understand that different kinds of messages call for different organizational patterns, we need to learn how to suit the way we say things to the type of message being sent and the organizational pattern most appropriate to that type of message. How to make the strategic choice as to the best writing style in a given situation will constitute, as you will see, the bulk of this book.

To orient ourselves to strategic style selection, let's consider some of the questions raised by the Scalpel case. In rejecting Scalpel, for example, we know that we want to be circuitous in organization. We want to prepare him emotionally for the rejection that is coming. We do not want to say 'Dear Frank: No!" But what style do we want to use?

- *Do we want to be forceful or passive in the way we express ourselves?*
  By using the passive voice constantly, version II precludes its author from ever having to say, "I must say no." Furthermore, the use of the passive in the sentence in version III, "it is felt that my services on the team could be construed," allows its author to imply that some mysterious *others* (not the writer) "could construe" Scalpel's request as inviting an improper conflict of interest. And the statement "it is felt" also hides the author far more that would the forceful "I feel." ("It is felt? Who felt it? Not me!")

- *Do we want to be personal or impersonal in our writing style?*
  Do we want to say "Dear Frank" (as does version II) or "Dear Mr. Scalpel" (as does version I)? Do we want to put further distance between ourselves and Scalpel by using the impersonal, legalistic phraseology and Latinate vocabulary of version I? Does version I's abstract, textbook-like diction make what is said seem less of a personal rejection of Scalpel? In short, is it strategically wise to be personal or impersonal in this case?

- *Is it wise to be colorful or colorless when responding to Scalpel?*
  Version IV is certainly colorful to the point of being breezy. The use of adjectives as in "sure-fire proposal" and "kind words," and the use of colorful figures of speech like "judge and advocate" and "give me a buzz" suggest that the author of version IV is intent on keeping everything light and hoping to brush the problem aside with a wave of the hand. Will this lighthearted manner work?

You can see how the answers to the questions raised in the previous paragraph will tell us what type of business writing style we should choose to use or avoid in this particular situation. And these questions should be asked about all messages you write. The choices for style that we will use in this book are:

- Forceful or passive?
- Personal or impersonal?
- Colorful or colorless?

Please bear in mind that these styles (as defined in the next section) are not mutually exclusive; there is some overlapping. A passive style is usually far more impersonal than it is personal, and it also is usually colorless. A forceful style is likely to be more personal than it is impersonal, and a colorful style is likely to be reasonably forceful. Even so, there is sufficient distinction among these styles to justify acting as if they were completely separate and distinct. If we fail to make such distinctions, *style* becomes a catchall word, meaning nothing specific.

In short, our choice of the terms *forceful, passive, personal, impersonal, colorful,* and *colorless* will prove to be extremely useful, even if not absolutely precise. These somewhat arbitrary distinctions allow us to talk about style and its elements and to learn how to write in a specific style in a given situation. For if we have no words with definitions, we cannot talk. We can only wave our arms around and make meaningless sounds, which, because of the lack of critical vocabulary about business writing style, is what generally goes on in offices all over the country.

# 5

## SIX KEY STYLES
## TO SUIT YOUR GOALS

Here are some suggestions as to how you can make your style more forceful or more passive; more personal or more impersonal; more colorful or colorless. And these suggestions serve also to define clearly each of these commonly used styles of business writing.

### FOR A FORCEFUL STYLE

A forceful style conveys courage and a sense of personal responsibility for what is being said. When used in the right situation, it is effective. When used at the wrong time, it can prove exceedingly harmful. Your style will be forceful if you:

- Use the active voice. Have your sentences do something to people and to objects, not just lie there having things done to them.
- Give orders—use the imperative.
  "Correct this error immediately" (*you*—understood—is the subject) instead of "A correction should be made" (which leaves the reader wondering, "Made by whom?").

- Step up front and be counted.
  "I have decided not to recommend you for promotion," instead of, "Unfortunately a positive recommendation on your promotion is not forthcoming."
- Do not beat around the bush or act like a politician. If something needs to be said, say it directly.
- Write most of your sentences in subject–verb–object order. Do not weaken sentences by putting namby-pamby phrases before the subject:
  "I have decided to fund your project," instead of, "After much deliberation and weighing of the pros and cons, I have decided to fund your project."
- Do not weaken sentences by relegating the point or the action to a subordinate clause.
  If your point is that your company has won a contract, say, "ABCD won the contract, although the bidding was intense and highly competitive," not "Although the bidding was intense and highly competitive, the contract was won by ABCD."
- Adopt a tone of confidence and surety about what you say by avoiding "weasel" words like:
  *possibly, maybe, perhaps, it could be concluded that ..., some might conclude that....*

---

### FOR A PASSIVE STYLE

A passive style (except in technical and scientific prose where its use is strictly conventional) conveys softness and a lack of blunt abrasiveness. When appropriately used, it can prove to be a valuable ally. Your style will be passive if you:

- Avoid the imperative—never give an order.
  Say, "A more effective and time-conserving presentation of ideas should be achieved before our next meeting," as opposed to, "Do a better job of presenting your ideas at our next meeting. Respect my time and get right to the point!"
- Use the passive-voice heavily, because the passive subordinates the subject to the end of the sentence (or buries the subject entirely). This is especially handy when you are in a lower power position and are forced to convey negative information to a reader who is in a higher position (such as an important customer).
  Say, "Resources are being wasted," instead of, "Resources are being wasted by your company," or even worse, "You are wasting resources."

- Avoid taking responsibility for negative statements by attributing them to faceless, impersonal "others."

    Say, "It is more than possible that several objections to your proposed plans might be raised by some observers..., or, "Several objections might be raised by those hostile to your plans" instead of, "I have several objections to your plans."

- Use "weasel words," especially if the reader is in a higher power position and will not like what you are saying.

- Use long sentences and heavy paragraphs to slow down reader comprehension of sensitive or negative information.

## FOR A PERSONAL STYLE

A personal style is one that sounds like one human being talking to another. It doesn't sound like a textbook. Perhaps this style should really be called a "personable" style, because it exudes charm and warmth. Your style will be personal if you:

- Use active voice, which puts you at the front of sentences.

    "I thank you very much," instead of, "Your comments were very much appreciated by me," or the even more impersonal, "Your comments were very much appreciated."

- Use people's names (first names, when appropriate) instead of referring to them by title.

    "Bill James attended the merger meeting," instead of, "ABCD's director attended the merger meeting."

- Use personal pronouns—especially *you* and *I*—when saying positive things.

    "I so much appreciate the work you've done," as opposed to, "What has been accomplished is appreciated."

- Use short sentences that capture the rhythm of ordinary conversation.

    "I discussed your proposal with Frank. He's all for it!" as opposed to, "This is to inform you that your proposal was taken up at Friday's meeting and that it was regarded with favor."

- Use contractions (*can't, won't, shouldn't*) to sound informal and conversational.

- Direct questions at the reader:

    "Just ask yourself. How would your company like to save $10,000?"

- Interject positive personal thoughts and references that will make the reader know that this letter is really to him or her, and not some type of form letter sent to just anyone.

## FOR AN IMPERSONAL STYLE

An impersonal style sounds like a textbook or a policy manual. It does not sound like a conversation. It is withdrawn and often cerebral. Your style will be impersonal if you:

- Avoid using people's names, especially first names. Refer to people (if at all) by title or job description.
- Avoid using personal pronouns, especially *I* and *you*. *(We* may be all right because the corporate *we* is faceless and impersonal.)
- Use the passive voice to make yourself conveniently disappear when desirable.
  Say, "A possible conclusion is that an error has been made in the calculations," instead of, "I think your calculations are wrong!"
- Make some of your sentences complex and some paragraphs long; avoid the brisk, direct, simple sentence style of conversation.

## FOR A COLORFUL STYLE

A colorful style usually conveys a literary quality, like poetry or an advertisement. If well used, it will increase the impact of your prose. Inappropriately used, it will make your business reader laugh at you. Figures of speech such as, "Where emerald seas kiss the golden sands," sound great in a travel brochure but ridiculous in a report dealing with a business trip. Your style will be colorful if you:

- Insert some adjectives and adverbs.
  Instead of, "This proposal will save corporate resources," write, "This (hard-hitting, productivity-building, money-saving) proposal will (easily, surely, quickly, immediately) save (hard-earned, increasingly scarce, carefully guarded) corporate resources."
- Use (if appropriate) metaphors (A is B), similes (A is like B), or other figures of speech to make a point.
  Write "This program is truly a miracle of design," or "This program is like magic in its ability to..."

## FOR A COLORLESS STYLE

A colorless style is dull and lacking in emotional impact on the reader. Your style will be colorless if you:

- Avoid using adjectives, adverbs, metaphors, similes, and other figures of speech.
- Blend an impersonal style with a passive style.
- Employ only formal words and expressions that best serve to freeze out any semblance of wit, liveliness, and vigor from the writing.

# 6

---

# HOW TO MASTER WRITING
# IN DIFFERENT STYLES

Now that we have defined the choices in business writing styles, we can meaningfully discuss drafts of important letters and memos. We don't need to wave our arms around and say, "I don't like the way you've said this! I won't sign it!"

Let's invent some typical business situations where you might find yourself having to shift from one style to another. As our first case, assume you have written the following draft and have shown it to your manager for approval.

*Version I*

TO:    All Headquarters Staff

FROM: Manager, Management Development Programs

Education is as important this year as any. Between now and the end of the month, make up a sound education plan for all members of your group. Remember, all staff must receive 30 hours of management training annually.

Feel free to come in and talk about your plan at any time. Turn in your plan by the end of the month; keep a copy handy and use it monthly to check your progress and modify it.

Give me your modifications.

Check your education plans against your vacation plans to make sure there are no conflicts.

After reading version I, your manager tells you to make it less forceful. It seems to her, rightly or wrongly, too pushy. You must revise according to her instructions. Applying what you've learned about various styles, you now can see clearly why your manager felt this memo was too forceful. Look at the stream of imperatives you've used:

- "Make up a sound education plan"
- "Remember, all staff must"
- "Feel free to come in"
- "Turn in your plan"
- "Keep a copy handy"
- "Use it monthly"
- "Give me your modifications"
- "Check your education plans"

What you have to do is use a style that does not give so many orders. On the other hand, you don't want the style to be completely passive because you are trying to motivate readers to take the actions you desire. Perhaps, instead of moving your style toward the passive, you should move it toward the personal. Perhaps you can create a draft that sounds as if you are talking with the staff members, not bossing them around.

*Version II*

TO:    All Headquarters Staff

FROM: Manager, Management Development Programs

Don't you agree that education is at least as important this year as any? So it's time for me to remind you to make up this year's education plans for all members of your group.

I will be available at any time to discuss your plans with you. And I'd find it especially helpful if your plan could be turned in to me by the end of the month.

Remember, it's always advisable to keep a copy of your plan handy so that you can refer to it monthly to check progress and make modifications. Remember also that these modifications should, of course, be shared with our office.

One final reminder: Check vacation plans against education plans to make sure there are no conflicts. Let me hear from you soon.

You compare version II with version I, and you agree that the revision is clearly superior. The imperatives (do this, do that) are gone. Yet none of the content has changed. Everything asked of the readers in the first draft is asked of them here. But there is a big difference between the styles of the two versions. You now agree with your manager; the style of the first version is inappropriately too forceful. The style of the second seems far warmer and more personal. It sounds like one colleague chatting with another. By changing your style, you have engineered a memo that will please both your manager and your readers. We say "engineered" because, thanks to your understanding of how to shift styles, you made stylistic improvements scientifically, not accidentally.

Next, assume that you have written the following draft of a letter encouraging your company's salespeople to invite appropriate customer personnel to attend a conference on current manufacturing problems. This conference is sponsored annually by your company.

*Version I*

TO:    All Sales Personnel

FROM: Sales Headquarters

A presentation will be made by Dr. J. R. Adelson of the London Institute of Technology at this year's Manufacturing Executive Conference to be held on October 27.

Efforts should be made to support this conference by encouraging attendance by appropriate customer personnel.

Brochures and enrollment instructions have been made available from Sales Headquarters, if desired.

You do not find the draft satisfactory in terms of being sufficiently forceful, personal, or colorful.

Let's see what can be done with this memo. You notice the following about the first draft, and decide on appropriate revisions.

*Original:*   It is expressed completely in the passive voice ("will be made," "should be made," "have been made").

*Revision:*   To make your memo forceful, you will use the active voice and include some imperatives.

*Original:*   It is completely impersonal; there are no personal pronouns and only one name (Dr. Adelson).

*Revision:*   You will make it personal by adding personal pronouns, and you will make it sound like a conversation with the readers, perhaps by adding a question directed toward them and evoking a response.

*Original:*   It is as flat and colorless as a dull textbook.

*Revision:*   To make it colorful, you will add adjectives and adverbs.

Here's what results from your efforts.

### *Version II*

TO:    All Sales Personnel

FROM: Sales Headquarters

Are you going to let your valued customers miss this year's exciting and innovative Manufacturing Executive Conference on October 27? Make sure you don't!

Tell them that the highlight of this important conference will be a stimulating presentation by the highly respected Dr. J. R. Adelson of London's renowned Institute of Technology.

Do everything you can to make this year's conference the biggest and best attended ever.

Attractive, informative brochures, available from my office, contain the simple enrollment instructions. Request as many brochures as you need. We will send them immediately for you to share with your customers.

You pause and analyze your revision.

1. Is it forceful? Yes. Four of the six sentences are imperatives ("Don't," "Tell," "Do," and "Request").

2. Is it personal? Yes. It begins conversationally with a question. It contains plenty of personal pronouns (*your, them, you, my, you,* and *your*). There is also an understood *you* in the imperatives, so these

four sentences also are addressed personally to the understood *you*, the reader.

3. Is it colorful? Yes. Adjectives abound. (Note the adjectives: *valued, exciting, innovative, important, stimulating, highly respected, renowned, biggest and best, attractive, informative, simple,* and an adverb, *immediately.*)

# 7

## THE BEST STYLE FOR YOU TO USE DEPENDS ON WHETHER YOU ARE WRITING UP OR DOWN

In order to judge how readers will react to your style, you have to concern yourself with your power position relative to your reader. Every thoughtful businessperson knows that the effectiveness of the way we say things depends not only on the type of message we are sending, but also on whether we are sending it up or down. Obviously, the more power a writer has over the reader, the less difference it makes just how the writer has said things. And, conversely, the less power a writer has over a reader, the more important it is for the writer to say things in a way that will affect the reader favorably.

### LOWER VERSUS HIGHER WRITING POSTURES

We will use the following definitions of higher and lower power positions:

42

- Writers are in a lower power position when they are writing *upward* to the reader, such as when writing to superiors in organizations, to powerful outside customers, or to total strangers who may simply throw the letter into the wastebasket.
- Writers are in a higher power position when they are writing *downward* to the reader, such as when writing to subordinates in organizations, or to a reader who is dependent upon the writer's good will—for example, a supplier primarily existing on the writer's business.

In order to learn something useful about what style is best to use in which power situation, we will experiment and see what we can learn together. Here is how we propose to set up our experiment.

1. We will focus on sample letters being written upward or downward in a power hierarchy. (Letters written laterally to equals will be dealt with later in section 14.)
2. These letters will include examples of the four types of messages discussed in the first section—negative, positive, persuasive, and information-conveying messages.
3. We will take each type of message and write a draft version in each of our three style choices—forceful versus passive, personal versus impersonal, and colorful versus colorless.

---

## ONLY THE STYLE VARIES IN THIS EXPERIMENT

All letters will be in response to hypothetical business cases. The content of each version will remain essentially the same; only the style will differ. In this way, we can hope to make some judgments about which style works best in each situation.

This approach, we feel, is far better than an approach in which we might reproduce actual business letters illustrative of the different styles. This would not be hard to do. But then each illustrative letter would be dealing with a different business situation and the versions would not be truly comparable.

Furthermore, so that we will be forced to concentrate on style only, we have written each version in the same organizational pattern. Because the direct pattern is more economical in terms of space—and less wasteful of your time—we have used the direct organizational pattern in all versions.

It is important that you heed this point: we have always used the direct organizational pattern regardless of whether that pattern most suits the type of message being sent.

Only in this way can readers be forced to admit that their reactions to various memos are caused by style changes, not by shifts in organizational pattern.

In every instance, we will write these versions to the very best of our ability. We will not intentionally burlesque a style or stack the deck in any way. Then we will assess the probable reception each of these versions might get from a reader. After each section, there will be a chart on which you can mark your reaction about the appropriateness of the style used. Once you have done so, we will share our reaction.

Remember, we have conducted extensive experimentation identical to the experiments we are embarking on here. Over 1,000 businesspeople and hundreds of college juniors and seniors have been given exactly the same tests you will take.

Obviously, we could just report our findings about how most people reacted to certain styles in various business situations. In short, we could simply play the expert and lecture you.

But our years of teaching have absolutely convinced us that the knowledge one discovers for oneself (even if the hard way) has a way of sticking with you, of being more remembered and used than is knowledge supposedly derived from lectures or sermons, or even from being yelled at. (If you doubt this, observe your children's learning patterns!)

That is why the case method of instruction is so popular at some leading graduate business schools. Cases involve students; they have to enter the case and *be* "Mr. Jones" or "Ms. Greggson" and make decisions.

Therefore, we ask you to enter into the cases that follow; let yourself react to the various styles of memos we concoct for different communication situations. Mark down your reactions. Then, compare them with ours and consider what we have to say.

Be assured that, later in this book, you will have a chance to compare your reactions—and ours—with those of the panels of businesspeople we have tested. And all of this knowledge will be summed up conveniently for you before we are through.

# 8

## SENDING NEGATIVE MESSAGES UP— YOUR MOST TOUCHY SITUATION

Negative messages written upward are the ones most likely to cause bad reactions from your readers. These are the messages in which the style used has the highest potential to cause trouble.

Let's invent a case in which a negative message must be sent up in an organization by a writer who is in a lower power position.

### Case

A product manager is obliged to respond to a request from the president of his corporation for written comments about a draft of a letter to stockholders. The final draft of the letter will be signed by the president and included in the company's annual report. The letter has been circulated to selected employees for their reactions. The product manager discovers some faults in the letter and decides he must share these concerns frankly with the president.

Which style of writing is best for the product manager to use?

---

## FORCEFUL VERSUS PASSIVE STYLE UPWARD

Version I of the product manager's letter illustrates the use of a highly forceful style of communication, and version II uses a passive style. How effective do you think each of these styles would be in this upwardly written but negative message?

*Version I—Forceful*

TO:    Corporation President

FROM: Product Manager

Here are my comments about the proposed letter to stockholders you circulated for employee reaction:

1. Don't come so close to a guarantee of increased profits in the fourth quarter. This is risky.
2. Stop being defensive about the company's performance this year. This insults those of us who worked as hard as we could.

*Version II—Passive*

TO:    Corporation President

FROM: Product Manager

In reference to your request for employee comments about the proposed stockholder letter, the following observations could be made.

A guarantee of increased profits in the fourth quarter seems to be implied, and, as a result, a possibly unnecessary risk may be incurred.

Also, a less defensive posture could be taken about the company's performance this year. Such a posture would be appreciated by most employees.

Think through how you feel a powerful reader would react to each of these versions. Then form a judgment as to the advisability or inadvisability of each style in this negative situation and with this powerful reader. Register your judgment by checking the appropriate blocks in the following chart.

| Negative Message Upward | | | | | |
|---|---|---|---|---|---|
| | Strongly Advis- able | Advis- able | Does Not Matter | Inadvis- able | Strongly Inad- visable |
| **Forceful** | | | | | |
| **Passive** | | | | | |

We're sure you see why version I is forceful. It gives commands. Its sentences are short and full of punch. In fact, it is so forceful that it is very brave, perhaps to the point of being foolhardy. We think it is safe to conclude that most prudent product managers would not write in this style to the presidents of their corporations.

Version II is clearly passive. Where version I's sentence structure is active and hence direct—subject–verb–object, version II's sentence structure is passive and hence indirect—object–verb–subject. The subject of a sentence is withheld until the end just as is the thrust of a message in the circuitous pattern of organization. Note the passive sentences:

"observations could be made"

"guarantee ... seems to be implied"

"risk may be incurred"

"posture could be taken"

"posture would be appreciated"

This passive style is possibly undesirable as a style of writing in general. On the other hand, it is also clearly safer in this particular situation, we would think, than is the forceful style of version I.

Just to make sure that we have a meeting of the minds about our experiment, let me remind you that we have no way of knowing whether your individual corporation president or your superior might, in fact, like the use of a forceful style in letters written to him or her. Nor do we know whether your personal relationship is one in which, over the years, your superior has developed such great confidence and trust in you that you feel completely free to write in as candid and blunt a fashion as you like.

But we strongly believe that, in general, when you or anyone else is writing from a lower power position to someone who is powerful (and with whom you do not enjoy the kind of personal confidence we mentioned above), you are far better off adopting a style of writing that is decidedly less forceful than version I.

Therefore, on our chart, we have checked the "strongly inadvisable" column about this forceful negative message written up. In fact, we would conclude, based on common sense and personal experience, that the lower the position writers hold when writing negative messages upward, the less forceful their style should be.

| Negative Message Upward | | | | | |
|---|---|---|---|---|---|
| | Strongly Advis- able | Advis- able | Does Not Matter | Inad- visable | Strongly Inadvis- able |
| **Forceful** | | | | | X |
| **Passive** | X | | | | |

## PERSONAL VERSUS IMPERSONAL STYLE UPWARD

Now let's see what conclusions we can draw about the impact of personal and impersonal styles in this same case of a negative message written up.

*Version I—Personal*

TO:     Corporation President

FROM: Product Manager

I would like to give you my comments about your proposed letter to stockholders, which you circulated for our reaction:

1. If I were you, I don't think I would want to appear to be making a personal guarantee of increased profits in the fourth quarter. None of us would like to see you run the risk of building false expectations among stockholders.

2. I think you should also ask yourself this question: How do you think your own employees will react to this letter, not just how stockholders will react? If you do, I think you will come to the conclusion that this draft of the letter makes you sound very defensive about all of our performances this year.

I know that I personally worked as hard as I could and I am
sure that goes for the rest of the employees.

I hope these comments prove helpful to you as you set about
deciding upon the final draft of the stockholder letter.

### Version II—Impersonal

TO:   Corporation President

FROM: Product Manager

Here are the requested comments about the proposed stockholder
letter:

1. There is an implied guarantee of fourth-quarter profits that
   could inadvertently build unfounded stockholder
   expectations.
2. There appears to be a note of defensiveness about this year's
   corporate performance that could adversely affect employee
   morale.

Again, decide how you feel a powerful reader would react to
each of these versions. Then, form a judgment about the
advisability or inadvisability of each style in this situation. Mark
your judgments on this chart.

| Negative Message Upward | | | | | |
|---|---|---|---|---|---|
| | Strongly Advis- able | Advis- able | Does Not Matter | Inadvis- able | Strongly Inadvis- able |
| **Personal** | | | | | |
| **Impersonal** | | | | | |

We're sure you felt that version I is about as warm and
personal a communication as it is possible to write. It is tactful
and constructive. But we imagine that you asked yourself this: Is
the intensely personal nature of this letter likely to cause a
negative reaction on the part of the reader? Is it appropriate for
someone at a lower level in a corporation to write so very
personally, even familiarly, to the president of the company?

And, even more important, is it wise to be so very personal
and warm and friendly when writing something that is negative
to the expectations of the reader, especially when that reader is
so very much the writer's superior?

Version II is all business. There are no personal pronouns or names. It is not conversational. It does not chattily pose questions to the reader. It simply and straightforwardly gets the job done. Sure, it conveys the same negative message as version I, but it does not do so in a personal way.

Our feeling was that a personal style of writing tends, by its very nature, to bring you, the writer, into the picture much more closely. As a result, a negative message becomes clearly identified with you. In other words, when you boil things down psychologically, a personal negative letter amounts to you personally telling the reader he or she is wrong; you are like the slave bringing Cleopatra the bad news and receiving an asp for your trouble.

In general, therefore, we would conclude that the more personal writers become in upward communications of negative messages, the more those writers may tend to worsen the situation for themselves. As a result, we have checked "strongly advisable" on impersonal style on our chart. And we have checked "strongly inadvisable" about a personal style being used in a negative message written up.

| Negative Message Upward | | | | | |
|---|---|---|---|---|---|
| | Strongly Advis- able | Advis- able | Does Not Matter | Inadvis- able | Strongly Inadvis- able |
| **Personal** | | | | | X |
| **Impersonal** | X | | | | |

## COLORFUL VERSUS COLORLESS STYLE UPWARD

Now let's consider our final style choice—a colorful versus colorless way of saying things—in this negative communication written up. We don't think we need a colorless version of this letter. Either the impersonal or the passive version can serve as illustrations. So let's simply be colorful.

TO:    Corporation President

FROM: Product Manager

Here is my frank feedback about the letter to stockholders you bucked around for comment:

1. Some hungry lawyer will surely pounce—like a cat on a mouse—on your seeming guarantee of increased fourth-quarter profits!
2. Why publicly cry the blues about this year's performance? Most of us feel like sticking our heads in the oven as it is!

How do you think a powerful reader would react to this version? Make a judgment about how wise it seems to you to be colorful in an upward negative situation. Then, come to a conclusion about how wise it probably is to be colorless in style. Check the appropriate blocks in the following chart.

| Negative Message Upward | | | | | |
|---|---|---|---|---|---|
| | Strongly Advis-able | Advis-able | Does Not Matter | Inadvis-able | Strongly Inadvis-able |
| **Colorful** | | | | | |
| **Colorless** | | | | | |

Of course, there is no way of guaranteeing that everybody will experience the same reaction to this colorful style. But we feel it is safe to conclude that most corporation presidents would not like to receive from a subordinate a letter written in this breezy, colorful style. The use of figures of speech such as "cat on a mouse" and "sticking our heads in the oven" only increases the impact this communication has on the reader. Since this situation is negative, why increase the negative impact?

You have checked how well you think a colorful style of writing would go over in your job situation. And you can compare your judgment with ours. We checked "strongly inadvisable" about the use of colorful writing in negative messages being written up. We think that being colorful will tend to worsen negative situations. As a result, we conclude that a colorless style is "strongly advisable."

| Negative Message Upward | | | | | |
|---|---|---|---|---|---|
| | Strongly Advis-able | Advis-able | Does Not Matter | Inadvis-able | Strongly Inadvis-able |
| **Colorful** | | | | | X |
| **Colorless** | X | | | | |

## CONCLUSIONS

So, as we consider our charts, we find that our conclusions about style in negative messages written up are that:

- It is very unwise to be forceful; therefore, we should find it strongly advisable to use a more passive style.
- It is also strongly inadvisable to adopt a personal style of writing in such situations, and it seems strongly advisable to write impersonally.
- It is strongly inadvisable to use a colorful style of writing in this situation, and it seems strongly advisable to employ a colorless style.

These conclusions are summarized in the chart below.

| Negative Message Upward | | | | | |
|---|---|---|---|---|---|
| | Strongly Advisable | Advisable | Does Not Matter | Inadvisable | Strongly Inadvisable |
| **Forceful** | | | | | X |
| **Passive** | X | | | | |
| **Personal** | | | | | X |
| **Impersonal** | X | | | | |
| **Colorful** | | | | | X |
| **Colorless** | X | | | | |

## TEST RUN

Let's put these conclusions to the test. See what you think about this final version of the same letter written in a passive, impersonal, and colorless style. If you believe this draft would go over well, then we think we have developed some practical generalizations about the appropriateness of various styles in upwardly written negative communication.

TO:    Corporation President

FROM: Product Manager

This is in response to your request for opinions relative to the proposed stockholder letter.

1. It is possible that some stockholders might draw the conclusion that a guarantee of fourth-quarter profits is being made. Perhaps some greater qualification of this statement might be considered.
2. It is also possible that some employees might feel that this draft places the company in the position of sounding defensive about our performance this year. A revision that reassures the stockholders of the dedication of all employees to a more profitable future might be more suitable to both internal and external audiences.

There it is. It is certainly far more passive than forceful. You will notice that we have avoided letting the writer accept personal responsibility for the negatives, by attributing all negative thoughts to faceless impersonal "others"—"some stockholders," "some employees." We have also weaseled very nicely by making everything conditional—"it is possible that...."

This version does not contain any colorful figures of speech or vivid adjectives, nor is it particularly personal. But it *is* safe. It does get the job done. And it should prove helpful to the president. If, on the other hand, the president violently disagrees with your observation, this style of letter has not exposed you personally to any great extent.

We suspect that more than a few readers are grumbling at this point, "I wouldn't weasel around like this. I'd say what I believe to anyone, no matter how powerful he or she is."

If you are one of these persons, all we can say is, "Congratulations!" You can be as brave as you want. But we ask you to put yourself in the position of offering general advice to many business people. Do you really want to encourage other possibly less experienced persons to convey negative messages to powerful readers in a forceful, personal, and possibly even colorful way? We doubt it. And, by the way, you may want to re-examine whether you are actually as blunt as you think you are. And, if so, whether that is wise.

# 9

## NEGATIVE MESSAGES SENT DOWN— DON'T SOUND LIKE CAPTAIN BLIGH

Now let's take up a situation where negative information must be conveyed downward from a writer in a position of power over the reader. In order to do so, we will have to alter our case. Let's assume that this is now the situation.

*Case*

The president of the corporation does not like the draft of the proposed letter to stockholders, which he is supposed to sign for inclusion in the annual report. Consequently, the president is conveying his negative feedback to his subordinate, the director of public relations, who is responsible for the draft.

### FORCEFUL VERSUS PASSIVE STYLE DOWNWARD

The first version of a letter written down from the president to the public relations director is in a forceful style. The second version is written in a more passive style. Note your reactions to each.

## Version I—Forceful

TO:    Public Relations Director

FROM: Corporation President

Here are my comments on the proposed letter to stockholders:
1. Don't make me sound as if I am almost guaranteeing increased profits in the fourth quarter. Too risky.
2. Don't make me sound so defensive about our performance this year. People in the company did the best they could, and they expect me to stand up for them to shareholders.

## Version II—Passive

TO:    Public Relations Director

FROM: Corporation President

After reading the draft of the proposed letter to stockholders and considering carefully its potential impact on investors as well as employees, certain observations can be made.

A guarantee of profits in the fourth quarter could be inferred by some readers and an unnecessary risk therefore run.

Similarly, a posture of defensiveness about the company's performance this year could be construed as casting negative aspersions on the efforts of all employees.

Which style do you think is more appropriate in this situation? Mark your reactions on this chart.

| Negative Message Downward | | | | | |
|---|---|---|---|---|---|
| | Strongly Advisable | Advisable | Does Not Matter | Inadvisable | Strongly Inadvisable |
| Forceful | | | | | |
| Passive | | | | | |

In version I, we're sure you noticed that the style is heightened by the use of the active voice rather than the passive, by the use of the imperative (giving orders), and by the use of short, punchy sentences and paragraphs.

By contrast, version II uses a passive, indirect (object–verb–subject) sentence structure. In fact, the first sentence illustrates a dangling participle because the subject (who is *reading* and *considering*) has been eliminated by the passive voice.

The writer is the president of the company, so he can write as forcefully as version I without necessarily causing a negative reaction in the reader. The reader already accepts the superiority of the writer's position and will probably simply set about revising the draft of the stockholder letter without strong emotional reaction.

Nevertheless, on our chart, we have checked "advisable" instead of "strongly advisable" for forceful style. Our feeling is that top executives can use as forceful a style as they want when writing down to a subordinate. But why be overbearing? They have nothing (usually) to prove by using too forceful a style.

On the other hand, how often is it wise for a superior to appear passive and lacking in force, as would be the case in version II? That is why we have checked "inadvisable" for the passive style. You may have checked "strongly inadvisable," and you may be right.

| Negative Message Downward | | | | | |
|---|---|---|---|---|---|
| | Strongly Advis- able | Advis- able | Does Not Matter | Inadvis- able | Strongly Inadvis- able |
| **Forceful** | | X | | | |
| **Passive** | | | | X | |

The test, we would think, is this. Ask yourself what impression you want to make when you are writing down to subordinates in your job situation. Do you want to seem forceful to the point of perhaps sounding bullying? We would doubt it. On the other hand, we're sure you would not want to appear as wishy-washy as does the executive in version II. We suspect that your conclusions and ours about the impact of a forceful style in a downwardly written communication are quite compatible.

## PERSONAL VERSUS IMPERSONAL STYLE DOWNWARD

Version I is a draft of a negative letter written down in a highly personal style. Version II is written in an impersonal style. See what you think of each.

*Version I—Personal*

TO:    Public Relations Director

FROM: Corporation President

You asked for my comments on a letter to stockholders you drafted:

1. Why do you make me sound as if I'm guaranteeing increased fourth-quarter profits? You must know that this is risky.
2. And why make me appear so defensive about our performance this year? You make it look as if I'm not standing up for all those people who work so hard in the company. Just ask yourself how Mary Jones in data processing or Harry Arnold in the mail room would react to this letter.

*Version II—Impersonal*

TO:    Public Relations Director

FROM: Corporation President

Comments on the proposed letter to stockholders are as follows:

1. It is risky to sound as if a guarantee of fourth-quarter profits is being made.
2. A less defensive posture about corporate performance this year seems advisable from the viewpoint of employee morale.

Mark your reactions to each style on this chart.

| Negative Message Downward | | | | | |
|---|---|---|---|---|---|
| | Strongly Advis-able | Advis-able | Does Not Matter | Inadvis-able | Strongly Inadvis-able |
| **Personal** | | | | | |
| **Impersonal** | | | | | |

You agree, we're sure, that version I is quite personal in style. Notice the heavy use of the pronoun *you*. Notice also how the use of individual names—*Mary Jones* and *Harry Arnold*—really personalizes how things are said. Notice how the use of questions makes it appear as if two people are actually talking to each other. All of these qualities of highly personal writing, however desirable they may be in many situations, seem to us to fall quite flat in a negative letter, even one written down in an organization.

Most top executives did not get to the top by being insensitive to the feelings of those with whom they work. And even if they actually could get away with writing a highly personal but negative message down in the organization, they would quickly recognize that to do so would be to run a certain risk. Just think of the times you've heard people say, "Now let's not get personal about this," or, "He took it personally and got angry."

A personal style almost by definition increases the probability of something negative being taken personally. Most top executives are reluctant to run this risk under most circumstances, and they are especially reluctant to do so in writing.

By contrast, version II is all business. It just states the facts coldly and impersonally. And, somehow, this coldness and impersonality seem actually to go over better than does the personal style of version I. For that reason we have checked "strongly inadvisable" on our chart for personal style and "strongly advisable" for impersonal. It is possible that you might feel that "strongly inadvisable" is too harsh a conclusion. But we very much doubt that you found yourself checking much higher than "inadvisable."

| Negative Message Downward | | | | | |
|---|---|---|---|---|---|
| | Strongly Advis- able | Advis- able | Does Not Matter | Inadvis- able | Strongly Inadvis- able |
| **Personal** | | | | | X |
| **Impersonal** | X | | | | |

## COLORFUL VERSUS COLORLESS STYLE DOWNWARD

Now let's suppose that the president decided he wanted his memo to the public relations person to be more colorful, like this draft. (Again, we think the passive and impersonal versions can serve as apt examples of a colorless style in this situation.)

TO:    Public Relations Director

FROM: Corporation President

You asked for my comments on the letter to stockholders you whipped up:

1. I'm not Santa Claus, you know. Maybe *he* can guarantee increased fourth-quarter profits, but I sure can't!
2. And then make me stop being Kris Kringle and turn me into Poor Nell, crying about how miserably we have done this year.

Come on, get my act together by getting *your* act together!

How advisable do you think it is to be colorful, as opposed to colorless, in style here? Mark your reactions on the chart.

| Negative Message Downward | | | | | |
| --- | --- | --- | --- | --- | --- |
| | Strongly Advisable | Advisable | Does Not Matter | Inadvisable | Strongly Inadvisable |
| Colorful | | | | | |
| Colorless | | | | | |

Did you think a highly colorful version like this could be recommended in this situation? We doubt it. In fact, we doubt that you or anyone else will like this version, even after taking into account the fact that if one is writing from a very strong power position, almost any style can get by (in the short run).

Negative situations are not usually occasions to be colorful about. Being colorful increases the impact on the reader through the use of stimulating adjectives, adverbs, and figures of speech. And this holds true whether one is in a position of low or high power. For this reason we have checked "strongly inadvisable" for colorful style and "strongly advisable" for colorless.

| Negative Message Downward | | | | | |
| --- | --- | --- | --- | --- | --- |
| | Strongly Advisable | Advisable | Does Not Matter | Inadvisable | Strongly Inadvisable |
| Colorful | | | | | X |
| Colorless | X | | | | |

The conclusion to be drawn, we think, is that colorful writing does not belong at all in negative situations—whether they are written up or down—unless you are deliberately trying to heighten the message's negative impact and are willing to pay the price.

---

## CONCLUSIONS

To sum up, we see that in negative messages written down, we (at least) have concluded that:

- It is advisable to be forceful, but probably not advisable to be too forceful. On the other hand, being passive in such situations does not seem appropriate either.
- It is strongly inadvisable to be personal in negative situations, and it is strongly advisable to be impersonal.
- It is strongly inadvisable to be colorful in negative situations, and it is strongly advisable to be colorless.

These conclusions are summarized in the chart below.

| Negative Message Downward | | | | | |
|---|---|---|---|---|---|
| | Strongly Advis-able | Advis-able | Does Not Matter | Inadvis-able | Strongly Inadvis-able |
| Forceful | | X | | | |
| Passive | | | | X | |
| Personal | | | | | X |
| Impersonal | X | | | | |
| Colorful | | | | | X |
| Colorless | X | | | | |

---

## TEST RUN

Let's see what a letter written by the corporation president to his public relations director might look like if it had followed the guidelines of our checklist and been somewhat forceful, impersonal, and colorless.

TO:   Public Relations Director

FROM: Corporation President

Please make the following changes in the draft of the proposed stockholder letter:

1. Eliminate the implied guarantee of profits in the fourth quarter. Too risky.
2. Revise the fourth paragraph where the tone seems defensive about our performance this year. Instead, reassure stockholders about the dedication of all employees to a more profitable future.

Note that this version captures much of what we felt to be desirable about the impersonal style, yet it is quite forceful because of its use of the imperative (eliminate this, revise that). These sentences give orders but make the *you* understood rather than spelled out. However, these orders are preceded by an important word—*please*—which alone serves to soften the forcefulness of the style. We think this letter should get the job done without offending the public relations director in any way.

# 10

## POSITIVE MESSAGES UP OR DOWN— GOOD NEWS FOR EVERYBODY!

Let's remind ourselves that we have accepted the dictionary definition of style as the way something is said, as distinguished from the substance of what is said. We have seen in negative situations that being told something unpleasant makes readers more sensitive about the style of the communication, about the way they have been told that unpleasant bit of news.

We think (and we feel sure you will, too) that just the reverse is true about positive messages. The favorable reaction produced in a reader by a good news message serves to decrease the potential a style has for producing a negative emotional reaction. If someone is told, "Yes, you got the raise," the recipient of the message doesn't really pay much attention to the style in which the good news is conveyed.

It does not seem to matter whether people are writing good news up or down in an organization; their style will probably have very little impact upon the reader, simply because the positive message overrides any negative tone the style could possibly produce. For example:

1. You can be forceful:
   "Don't change a word! I like it as it is."
2. You can be personal:
   "Let me congratulate you on this draft, Joe. It's the best you've ever done."
3. You can be colorful:
   "This draft has punch and vitality. It will have the stockholders dancing in the aisles."

Let us see whether being forceful, personal, and colorful in positive messages is preferable to being passive, impersonal, and colorless—regardless of whether you are writing that positive message up or down.

Let's write a positive message down—the perfect situation, good news being sent from a writer in a higher power position. All aspects are favorable, right? But let's write this letter in a passive, impersonal, and colorless style. In other words, we will write a draft that will completely violate the temporary judgment we just made. What impression do you think the following draft would make?

TO:    Public Relations Director

FROM: Corporation President

Comments about the proposed stockholder letter are the following:

1. A favorable reaction by stockholders probably will be produced by this approach.
2. It is also likely that no negative employee reaction will occur.

We're sure you agree that this version is so passive, impersonal, and colorless that it almost succeeds in negating the positive message of the communication. Yet this effect wasn't easy to achieve; we had to work at it.

It seems inconceivable that such a passive, impersonal, color-less style would ever be used by a president writing down to a public relations director. Persons this timid about expressing themselves would be unlikely to be in a position of significant power.

---

## CONCLUSIONS

Now let's go to our chart and crystallize the conclusions we have drawn about positive messages written up or down. As far as forcefulness is concerned, we think (and we're sure you agree) that there is no reason not to be as forceful as you want, and that it is clearly inadvisable to be passive in both situations. We think it far more advisable to be personal than to be impersonal in writing a positive message up or down. Therefore, we've checked "strongly advisable" as well as "advisable" on both forceful and personal. And while it probably doesn't matter whether a positive message sent up or down is colorful or not, in some circumstances a colorful message may well be advisable. Therefore, we've checked both "doesn't matter" and "advisable" on colorful (to signify "possibly advisable"), and "doesn't matter" on colorless.

| Positive Message Upward or Downward | | | | | |
|---|---|---|---|---|---|
| | Strongly Advis-able | Advis-able | Does Not Matter | Inadvis-able | Strongly Inadvis-able |
| **Forceful** | X | X | | | |
| **Passive** | | | | X | X |
| **Personal** | X | X | | | |
| **Impersonal** | | | | X | X |
| **Colorful** | | X | X | | |
| **Colorless** | | | X | | |

We recognize that more than one check beside a given style seems confusing. But we don't know how else to signify that in positive messages it often doesn't really matter what style is used to convey the good news. So how can we insist, say, that it is strongly advisable to be forceful? It might not matter a great deal if the style were not forceful at all. But we do want to leave with you the idea that it is clearly preferable to be forceful when telling good news. For that reason, we have checked both "advisable" and "strongly advisable" columns.

So, too, if we seem to be waffling between strongly advisable and advisable on personal styles, it's for the same reason. The same holds true about our reaction to being colorful. It might add something to the good news message. But the absence of colorful style probably would never be noticed.

# 11

## WHAT STYLE BEST PERSUADES RELUCTANT SUBORDINATES TO DO WHAT YOU WANT?

In this discussion of style, we have found it extremely important to consider whether the writer is writing from a higher power position or a lower power position. Nowhere is this distinction more necessary than in the area of persuasive situations, where you need to talk readers into doing what you want them to do, whether they want to do it or not. If we were to assume that the writer has total power, then writers need merely state what they want—give an order, and it will be instantly obeyed. It really doesn't matter what kind of style is used in such a communication because readers are going to respond and do what they're asked, whether they like it or not.

However, we seldom have total power over those to whom we write. Therefore, you must be concerned about whether or not your readers will be persuaded favorably by the way you say things. Consequently, you need to learn something about the effectiveness of various styles in persuasive situations.

There are, of course, a multitude of persuasive situations, but if you think about them, they seem to break down into the following three basic categories:

1. *Negative persuasive situations,* in which the writer's task is to persuade readers to do something they don't want to do, something they perceive as being negative to their interests (regardless of how good it might be to their interests ultimately, like quitting smoking). Falling into this category are messages in which a superior resorts to attempts at persuading subordinates to do what is right because the superior chooses for various reasons not to make the request an order. (For example, a letter from a superior urging participation in the United Fund Campaign, or a Red Cross blood drive.)

2. *Positive persuasive situations,* in which what is requested is clearly positive (or at worst neutral) to the reader's interests. (We will define these later.)

3. *Blind persuasive situations,* in which the writer has no knowledge about the readers and must attempt to persuade them to do something they may either like or dislike.

Let's first take up negative persuasive messages downward through a case situation where readers are being asked to do something that implies a criticism of their behavior and is hence negative. The communication is from a person in a higher power position to a person in lower power.

### Case

The executive vice-president writes to all headquarters department managers urging them to set a good example for other employees by being more punctual about reporting to work and quitting. However, since this is a first reminder, and since some readers may, in fact, be innocent, the vice-president does not choose to issue a "now hear this" type of order.

## FORCEFUL VERSUS PASSIVE

Let's begin by comparing two versions of letters written by the executive vice-president—the first highly forceful and the second much more passive in style.

*Version I—Forceful*

TO:     All Headquarters Department Managers

FROM: Executive Vice-President

I strongly urge each of you to set a good example for your
subordinates by:
    1. Reporting to work on time each day, and
    —coor2. Not quitting until 5:00 P.M. or later.
I request your complete cooperation.

*Version II—Passive*

TO:     All Headquarters Department Managers

FROM: Executive Vice-President

A good example will be set for subordinates if superiors report to
work on time and depart not before 5:00 P.M. Expected will be full
cooperation.

How advisable is it to be forceful, as opposed to passive, in
style here? Mark your judgments on this chart.

| Negative Persuasive Message Downward | | | | | |
|---|---|---|---|---|---|
| | Strongly Advis- able | Advis- able | Does Not Matter | Inadvis- able | Strongly Inadvis- able |
| **Forceful** | | | | | |
| **Passive** | | | | | |

The forceful style of version I produces the tone of a top
executive coming very close to issuing a formal order. The words
*strongly urge* and *expect* leave little doubt in the minds of readers
that they had better pay attention. Furthermore, the indenta-
tions and short sentences increase the impact of the letter. The
use of the pronoun *I* at the beginning of each sentence makes it
clear that the higher-level executive is personally making this
request.

The passive style of version II has some appeal because our
case has stated that the executive vice-president does not want to
make this a "now hear this" type of communication. On the other
hand, version II makes the executive vice-president seem to be
so lacking in force, so reluctant to step up front and be counted,

that we doubt if most top executives would sign this passive version.

But if we want to be forceful in style, just how forceful should we be in a downward persuasive negative request? Let us consider the situation of our case. Keep in mind that this is the first letter that has been sent out to the managers. If it were the third time the higher-level executive had to make such a request, obviously it would call for a highly forceful style.

Therefore, what we can conclude is this. When you are making a downward negative persuasive communication, it might be well to be a bit lacking in forcefulness in the first communication but to increase the amount of forcefulness in the style of each subsequent communication. For that reason we have checked "advisable" instead of "strongly advisable" on forcefulness, and "inadvisable" on passive style.

| Negative Persuasive Message Downward | | | | | |
|---|---|---|---|---|---|
| | Strongly Advisable | Advisable | Does Not Matter | Inadvisable | Strongly Inadvisable |
| Forceful | | X | | | |
| Passive | | | | X | |

## PERSONAL VERSUS IMPERSONAL

Now let's ask ourselves how this persuasive message might fare if it had been written in a style that was personal (as in version I) or impersonal (as in version II).

*Version I—Personal*

TO:    All Headquarters Department Managers

FROM: Executive Vice-President

How do you think you would feel if your boss consistently reported to work later than you? Then made matters worse by leaving early? Not very good, I suspect.

Therefore, I know you will do all you can to set a good example for the people who report to you. In this tight economy, you and your fellow workers will want to make your contributions to our company's efficiency and productivity.

*Version II—Impersonal*

TO:    All Headquarters Department Managers

FROM: Executive Vice-President

The punctuality with which management reports to work in the morning and leaves at night sets an example for subordinates. Therefore, the announced beginning and ending times of work should be closely observed so as to make clear to subordinates that punctuality is basic to a well-run organization.

Mark your reactions to the two versions on this chart.

| Negative Persuasive Message Downward | | | | | |
|---|---|---|---|---|---|
| | Strongly Advis- able | Advis- able | Does Not Matter | Inadvis- able | Strongly Inadvis- able |
| **Personal** | | | | | |
| **Impersonal** | | | | | |

Version I is actually a well-written letter. But didn't you think the addition of personal, conversational qualities served to weaken the persuasiveness of the letter? We thought so. The personal style makes the memo sound more like a person actually lecturing the reader. You can almost see the writer shaking his finger at the reader. Readers will not feel that version I is a routine, general reminder. They will feel it is aimed at them personally.

What about version II? Here the impersonality decreases the likelihood of readers feeling themselves being personally scolded. And as a first communication it might well be strategic not to be so personal. Naturally, if no action results from a first letter, the vice-president would probably take sterner measures—indeed he might decide to become personal. (Whether he would do this in writing is, of course, another matter.)

Obviously, you are going to have to draw your own conclusions, based on your own work conditions and on each situation as it arises. But we feel it is safe to conclude that being impersonal is advisable and being personal is inadvisable or even strongly inadvisable in this type of downward negative persuasive communication.

| Negative Persuasive Message Downward | | | | | |
|---|---|---|---|---|---|
| | Strongly Advis- able | Advis- able | Does Not Matter | Inadvis- able | Strongly Inadvis- able |
| **Personal** | | | | X | X |
| **Impersonal** | | X | | | |

## COLORFUL VERSUS COLORLESS

Suppose, however, the executive vice-president wondered whether or not a colorful style of writing would prove to be more effective in this situation. Consider the following draft. (We do not need a sample of a colorless version, the less forceful and the impersonal versions from before can serve as illustrations.)

TO:    All Headquarters Managers

FROM: Executive Vice-President

Chaucer put it well: "If gold will rust, what will iron do?"

High-level management must set a golden example for subordinates. Are we doing so?

Are we having that extra cup of coffee in the mornings? And showing up late as a result? Are we thinking so much about an afternoon nine holes that we are leaving early?

These are tough economic times, and unless we lead by example we are not going to encourage the high productivity and efficiency that have made our company great.

What are your judgments?

| Negative Persuasive Message Downward | | | | | |
|---|---|---|---|---|---|
| | Strongly Advis- able | Advis- able | Does Not Matter | Inadvis- able | Strongly Inadvis- able |
| **Colorful** | | | | | |
| **Colorless** | | | | | |

How do you think most people would react to this letter? We can only judge from our own reactions. Our reaction, frankly, was somewhat ambivalent. For the first time in our discussion of style, a colorful style of writing did not seem completely inappropriate.

Our impression is that this colorful version has some possibilities of being effective especially when we remember that it is the first in a series. It exudes a certain amount of tact, possibly because its colorful style imparts an almost literary tone that makes the negative aspects of the message seem more abstract and less personal. Readers may admire the writing so much that they pay less attention to the negative message.

On the other hand, we recognize, as we're sure you do, that a colorful style employed in business situations runs a definite risk of appearing phony, overblown, and pretentious—even in advertisements, where a colorful style is commonplace.

But the most damaging argument against this colorful version is that most top executives would definitely not want to put their signature to this letter (or to any letter like it), no matter how much they might admire its literary style. For that reason, we have checked "inadvisable" on our chart for colorful and "advisable" for colorless.

| Negative Persuasive Message Downward | | | | | |
|---|---|---|---|---|---|
| | Strongly Advis-able | Advis-able | Does Not Matter | Inadvis-able | Strongly Inadvis-able |
| **Colorful** | | | | X | |
| **Colorless** | | X | | | |

## CONCLUSIONS

Here is a summary of our reactions to negative persuasive message sent down.

| Negative Persuasive Message Downward | | | | | |
|---|---|---|---|---|---|
| | Strongly Advis-able | Advis-able | Does Not Matter | Inadvis-able | Strongly Inadvis-able |
| **Forceful** | | X | | | |
| **Passive** | | | | X | |
| **Personal** | | | | X | X |

| | | | | |
|---|---|---|---|---|
| **Impersonal** | | X | | | |
| **Colorful** | | | | X | |
| **Colorless** | | X | | | |

We have suggested that a person probably would never (for image reasons) write downward in a strongly passive style. Therefore, being somewhat forceful is the recommendation. And because being personal or colorful in a negative situation will probably adversely affect the reader, an impersonal and colorless style is probably preferable.

# 12

## HOW TO PERSUADE SUPERIORS TO DO WHAT THEY DON'T WANT TO DO

Now let's reverse the situation and deal with negative persuasive communications written up. Here is the case situation we will use.

*Case*

A lower-level employee writes to the vice-president to request that he force headquarters office managers to obey the rules about starting and quitting times.

### FORCEFUL VERSUS PASSIVE

The lower-level employee is writing upward in a highly forceful style in version I and in a passive style in version II. How effective do you think each style would be in persuading the vice-president to take the requested action?

## *Version I—Forceful*

TO:    Vice-President

FROM: Lower-Level Employee

You owe it to all of us who report to work on time to make sure that our managers do so also. Take it from me, they don't!

Many regularly arrive an hour or two late. Also, some simply drift off an hour or more before the announced quitting time.

And don't let them tell you it's because they worked late the nights before. They didn't!

I'm sorry to be so blunt about this, but I'm sure I'm not the only one who thinks you should take strong and immediate action.

## *Version II—Passive*

TO:    Vice-President

FROM: Lower-Level Employee

This is a request that a study be made of the punctuality of our management—when they report to work and when they leave. There is the perception that many managers report late and leave early and that late work hours the night before is not a valid excuse.

If that study indicates that some reminders should be issued, the appropriate steps will be appreciated by me and, I'm sure, many others.

Mark your judgments of these two versions on the chart.

| **Negative Persuasive Message Upward** | | | | | |
|---|---|---|---|---|---|
| | Strongly Advis-able | Advis-able | Does Not Matter | Inadvis-able | Strongly Inadvis-able |
| **Forceful** | | | | | |
| **Passive** | | | | | |

How persuasive will the forceful style of version I probably be? By being so forceful in style, the lower-level employee seems to run the risk of raising a question in the superior's mind: "Who does this person think is boss around here?" This style definitely makes the superior feel as if he is being called on the carpet.

It seems to us that such a forceful style is highly inappropriate and almost suicidal. It definitely is not persuasive, when written up.

As weak and passive as version II is in style, didn't you think it is actually far more likely to be effective with the vice-president than the forceful version will be? The softness and lack of force in this letter impart a tone of tactfulness and respectfulness. It certainly does not raise the issue of "Who's the boss around here?" We think the superior will feel far less defensive and less threatened by the style of version II than the style of version I.

This again, however, reveals an instance where a great deal depends on one's relationship with a superior and on the environment in which work is done. There are work situations and bosses who really do like to be told things straight out. There are even more bosses who say they do but actually get their feathers ruffled by undiplomatic approaches such as that taken in version I.

After considering carefully, we've decided that a forceful style in a negative persuasive message written up is strongly inadvisable. And a passive style is strongly advisable. But what is of practical importance is *your* judgment about which style is best for you, in your work situation and with your boss.

| Negative Persuasive Message Upward | | | | | |
|---|---|---|---|---|---|
| | Strongly Advis- able | Advis- able | Does Not Matter | Inadvis- able | Strongly Inadvis- able |
| **Forceful** | | | | | X |
| **Passive** | X | | | | |

## PERSONAL VERSUS IMPERSONAL

Now let's see what happens when the lower-level person writes to the vice-president in a personal style as in version I, and in an impersonal style as in version II.

*Version I—Personal*

TO:     Vice-President

FROM: Lower-Level Employee

I want to make a serious request of you. And I believe that there may be many other rank-and-file employees who feel just as strongly as I do.

Please pay personal attention to when our managers report to work and when they leave. Then ask yourself this: Do these managers need a reminder of what our starting and quitting times actually are?

And please don't assume that these managers arrive late because they work late. No, some are coming in late and leaving early day after day.

Please look into this situation.

### Version II—Impersonal

TO:     Vice-President

FROM: Lower-Level Employee

The purpose of this memo is to request that a study be made of the punctuality of management in terms of both their reporting time and their time of leaving for the day.

Late arrival can be justified for some on the basis of having worked late the night before. However, for others the norm has become late arrival and early departure on the same day.

If this study indicates, as is probable, that action should be taken, such action will be appreciated.

Mark your judgments of the two versions on this chart.

| Negative Persuasive Message Upward | | | | | |
|---|---|---|---|---|---|
| | Strongly Advis-able | Advis-able | Does Not Matter | Inadvis-able | Strongly Inadvis-able |
| **Personal** | | | | | |
| **Impersonal** | | | | | |

Which style did you find more effective? Our feeling is that the impersonal style is far more effective than the personal style. In our experience, negative messages and a personal style simply do not seem to mix. We'll have more to say about this in section 20. At any rate, we have checked "strongly inadvisable" for personal style and "strongly advisable" for impersonal.

| Negative Persuasive Message Upward | | | | | |
|---|---|---|---|---|---|
| | Strongly Advis-able | Advis-able | Does Not Matter | Inadvis-able | Strongly Inadvis-able |
| **Personal** | | | | | X |
| **Impersonal** | X | | | | |

## COLORFUL VERSUS COLORLESS

Now let's try a highly colorful version of a letter for this case. (We do not need a sample of a colorless version; the less forceful and the impersonal versions from before can serve as illustrations.)

TO:     Vice-President

FROM: Lower-Level Employee

Why should managers get away scot free coming to work late and leaving early? Rules are made for everybody.

Some of our bosses are keeping banker's hours in the morning and golfer's hours in the afternoon.

And the old excuse of having to work late the night before is just hogwash in many cases!

The rest of us second-class citizens have gotten upset enough to ask me to blow the whistle.

What are your judgments?

| Negative Persuasive Message Upward | | | | | |
|---|---|---|---|---|---|
| | Strongly Advis-able | Advis-able | Does Not Matter | Inadvis-able | Strongly Inadvis-able |
| **Colorful** | | | | | |
| **Colorless** | | | | | |

We suspect that you will agree with us that being colorful in a serious business situation is not effective. In this situation, the superior is being asked essentially to start doing his job. The trick, therefore, is to couch that rather insulting request in a style that better enables the request to be granted. Being colorful imparts a frivolous, breezy tone, which, in most cases, will consciously or subconsciously annoy the superior. For that reason, we have checked the "strongly inadvisable" column on our chart.

| Negative Persuasive Message Upward | | | | | |
|---|---|---|---|---|---|
| | Strongly Advis-able | Advis-able | Does Not Matter | Inadvis-able | Strongly Inadvis-able |
| **Colorful** | | | | | X |
| **Colorless** | X | | | | |

## CONCLUSIONS

| Negative Persuasive Message Upward | | | | | |
|---|---|---|---|---|---|
| | Strongly Advis-able | Advis-able | Does Not Matter | Inadvis-able | Strongly Inadvis-able |
| **Forceful** | | | | | X |
| **Passive** | X | | | | |
| **Personal** | | | | | X |
| **Impersonal** | X | | | | |
| **Colorful** | | | | | X |
| **Colorless** | X | | | | |

In short, if you are trying to persuade higher-level people to do what *you* want, not what *they* want, write in a very low-key fashion. Be passive, impersonal, and colorless—and hope that the facts alone will persuade them to do what you ask.

# 13

## PERSUADING READERS TO DO WHAT'S GOOD FOR THEM IS EASY— BUT WHICH STYLES WORK BEST IN POSITIVE PERSUASION?

The second basic category of persuasive situations deals with communications where readers are being urged to do something positive, something that is clearly in their best interests. Let's make up a few examples:

*Down*

1. A memo to all employees urging them to get their flu shots from the clinic.
2. A letter to all middle managers reminding them that it is company policy for them to take annual vacations and for them to make their plans known to headquarters by April 30.

*Up*

1. A letter to an important customer urging her to place any orders before October 1 when a price increase is to go into effect.

2. A memo to your boss informing him that your analysis of the data supports his position and urging him to take the action you know he wants to take.

In positive persuasive situations like these, it seems obvious to us that this type of message does not differ from any other positive communication as far as appropriate style is concerned. In our analysis of positive messages, we concluded that:

1. It makes no difference whether the message is written up or down.
2. A forceful, personal, and possibly even colorful style is preferable to the reverse.

Our feeling is that the same conclusions hold true for positive persuasive messages, whether upward or downward. For example:

Don't run risks with your health this winter. Go to the clinic and get your flu shot.
Don't delay. Do it today!"

OR

Be sure to place any orders before October 1. I've just been informed that a price increase will go into effect at that time.

Since the readers can only be pleased that you are urging them to do something pleasant, or at least something that is good for them, why not use the same style that seemed effective in positive messages of a nonpersuasive nature?

Think of a few examples from your own environment and see whether you agree with our conclusions on the chart.

| Positive Persuasive Message Upward or Downward | | | | | |
|---|---|---|---|---|---|
| | Strongly Advis-able | Advis-able | Does Not Matter | Inadvis-able | Strongly Inadvis-able |
| **Forceful** | X | | | | |
| **Passive** | | | | | X |
| **Personal** | X | | | | |
| **Impersonal** | | | | | X |
| **Colorful** | | X | | | |
| **Colorless** | | | | X | |

Again, as in the case of positive messages, style does not matter as much as it does in negative messages. Therefore, while we advise being forceful, personal, and perhaps even colorful, not being so is not a matter of life or death.

On the other hand, we feel that writers need to be more forceful, personal, and probably more colorful when they are trying to persuade people to do something—even when that something is good for them. Hence, our checkmarks on positive persuasive are on stronger categories than they were on straight positive messages. Telling someone he or she got a raise is different from persuading someone to get a flu shot, and it requires a more forceful, personal, and colorful style.

# 14

---

# BLIND PERSUASIVE MESSAGES— STYLE CUES FROM MADISON AVENUE

The final basic category of persuasive situations includes those in which writers have no idea (other than perhaps some statistical probabilities based on the type of mailing list used) whether what is being asked will be received in a positive or negative way by the reader. Obviously, in such situations a lot more than just style is involved in a successfully persuasive letter. Writers have to:

1. Try to make readers believe that the action requested is in their best interests.
2. Offer convincing evidence (or arguments) to prove their assertions.

Every textbook on direct mail would agree with these points.

Now, if this is so, what conclusions can we make about style in a blind persuasive communication? It seems clear to us that if writers have to convince readers that the action requested is positive to their interests, writers should employ the style appropriate to a positive persuasive letter. That is, they should be:

1. *Forceful.* Why not? If the writer's style suggests passivity about the action requested, isn't that damaging to the success of the letter?

2. *Personal.* There are limits to how personal a writer can really get in a blind persuasive situation. However, the following qualities of a personal style are found in most direct mail communications:

   • Use of the personal pronoun *you* in general, especially to focus on what's in it for you.

   • Use of questions: "How would you like...?"

   • Use of people's names: Testimonials and endorsements by stars, and so on.

   • Use of a conversational style: Contractions *(wouldn't)* and short sentences and paragraphs.

3. *Colorful.* This is the one place where colorful writing is appropriate. There seems to be no need for us to rediscover what advertising people have known for centuries. ("Sail away 'neath star-filled skies to an isle where emerald seas kiss the golden sands....")

And it doesn't matter whether the message is being written upward or downward.

---

## CONCLUSIONS

All we have to do is read a few advertisements to find empirical proof that our conclusions about style hold water in the real world. We have marked our judgments on the following chart. As you see, they are identical to our judgments about positive persuasive letters upward or downward.

| Blind Persuasive Messages Upward or Downward | | | | | |
|---|---|---|---|---|---|
| | Strongly Advis-able | Advis-able | Does Not Matter | Inadvis-able | Strongly Inadvis-able |
| **Forceful** | X | | | | |
| **Passive** | | | | | X |
| **Personal** | X | | | | |
| **Impersonal** | | | | | X |
| **Colorful** | X | | | | |
| **Colorless** | | | | | X |

# 15

---

## WHAT STYLE WORKS BEST WHEN SIMPLY GIVING THE PRICE OF LEFT-HANDED WIDGETS?

Messages that simply convey nonsensitive information constitute the vast majority of letters and reports written by businesspeople. Fortunately, they are also the easiest type of communication to compose. Since there is no sensitivity involved, and since you are not trying to sell somebody something, you can use a very direct pattern of organization. And there is no reason not to use a writing style that is equally as direct.

If what we've put on our charts in the other situations is correct, we should be able to deduce from those conclusions the most effective writing style for conveying nonsensitive information in the general business situation. Remember, when the information is nonsensitive, it matters little whether the communication is sent up or down. The object is simply to get the information across in as businesslike a fashion as possible.

Our previous charts show that, in general, it is better to be reasonably forceful and to be appropriately personal. But we have seen that being colorful usually contributes nothing positive to most communications. And we have seen that the only time being colorless, passive, and impersonal seems appropriate is when we are dealing with highly sensitive, usually negative situations.

Nonsensitive, information-conveying messages obviously are not negative. So why not use the style of the positive message? If we do, the style of writing of an experienced business executive would be:

- As forceful as a situation will allow.
- As personal as seems appropriate.
- Colorful only in those *rare* situations where colorful writing is called for.

The following chart is marked appropriately.

| Information-Conveying Messages Upward or Downward | | | | | |
|---|---|---|---|---|---|
| | Strongly Advis- able | Advis- able | Does Not Matter | Inadvis- able | Strongly Inadvis- able |
| Forceful | | X | | | |
| Passive | | | X | X | |
| Personal | | X | X | | |
| Impersonal | | | X | X | |
| Colorful | | | X | | |
| Colorless | | X | X | | |

Note the strange pattern taken by our checks on this chart. Most checks fall in the middle range, around "doesn't matter." For the most part style doesn't really matter when one is relaying the fact that "the price of Model D–4 is $125.25." We merely have to look at the bulk of routine correspondence in most companies' files to know that people don't get fired for writing in a passive, impersonal style. But, perhaps, neither do they get rapid promotions. Therefore, we recommend that in nonsensitive, strictly information-conveying messages, you write the way successful, confident businesspeople do. Specifically:

- Get directly to the point and quit.
- Write forcefully.
  Use short, subject–verb–object sentences.

Use short paragraphs.
Use active voice always.
Use ordinary words.

- Write as personally as the situation allows.

 Use first names, names, and personal pronouns.
 Use the rhythms of conversation, make what you write sound as if you are speaking directly to the reader.

- Go easy on the use of colorful style. Too many colorful adjectives, adverbs, and figures of speech will seem highly inappropriate.

## DO AS THE ROMANS DO

We recognize that you exist in a particular environment on your job. And you must conform to that environment's expectations. If, for example, you are an engineer, we know you would be foolish indeed to write an engineering report in the style that we recommend for general business use. If you did, your readers—probably also engineers—would probably find your style inappropriate and somewhat distasteful. It would not be the way things are said in your discipline.

Or, if your occupation lies in the colorful, creative advertising world, for you to write in a style that avoids colorful turns of phrase and bluntly blurts out "do this; do that," might well evoke a negative reaction from your peers. Only *you* can best judge the style of writing that is appropriate in the shop-talk of your job environment.

But is this a reason for not becoming proficient in the general business style of writing? Absolutely not. As you rise in the hierarchy of your organization, you will need to be proficient in the style of writing employed by most higher-level executives when they convey nonsensitive information throughout the organization. If you write like a technician then, it will jar. If your style sounds too literary, or too much like ad copy, it will be laughed at.

Remember, most of what you write is strictly for the purpose of conveying information. Why not convey that information in the style used by most high-level executives?

But also remember that while the majority of your writing may be nonsensitive, it is the sensitive communication that will cause you the most trouble and may, if poorly handled, cause you the most grief. Don't write sensitive messages (especially up) in the forceful, personal style of the top executive writing down.

# 16

## THE WHEEL OF STYLE: YOUR DESK-DRAWER GUIDE TO SUCCESSFUL WRITING

As this book has unfolded, we have documented how we would most probably react to certain styles of writing in relation to different messages and varying reader and writer power positions. But we constitute a ludicrously small sample. The question we beg is this: Are our reactions typical of the reactions of average businesspeople?

Naturally, we can't answer for you. But our reactions did turn out to be quite typical of those expressed by experienced businessmen and businesswomen. (Yes, there were no differences in the way men and women reacted.)

To obtain these reactions, we carried out the following experiment over a period of time with small groups (usually 20 to 25 persons) of businesspeople of varying ages, and later with large groups of juniors and seniors in a business school. The subject groups totaled 1,104 businesspeople and 396 college students. The percentage of males was slightly larger in the business group; in the college group the percentages were about equal.

The experiments were carried out by showing all subjects slides of each of our cases and our various draft versions of memos, exactly as was done in this book. Each subject was given a blank chart on which to note his or her reaction to each version. No sharing of reactions was allowed until all responses to each case (such as negative messages upward) had been given. Then the subjects were polled as to how they reacted, and a summary total of their responses was taken for later comparison.

When all message types, up or down, were shown, and all responses given, the votes for all subjects in all groups were pooled and tallied. These subjects' responses were then compared with the recommendations we made in the previous chapters. In every instance we found that the vast majority of voters agreed with our predictions. In most instances the rate of agreement was virtually 100 percent; it was never below 80 percent.

We think it's fair to conclude that we now know which styles are most likely to produce the desired effect on a reader who is receiving a given type of message. That is knowing a lot, but it is not knowing everything. We still need to decide which type of organizational pattern is called for in that situation.

The organizational pattern that best suits each type of message has been discussed briefly in section 3 of this book and has been analyzed in depth in *Bottom-Line Business Writing*,* another volume in this series. That analysis concluded as follows:

1. *The bottom-line (or direct) pattern,* in which the message is bluntly and immediately expressed, should be used in:

   • Information-conveying messages upward or downward
   • Positive messages upward or downward
   • Positive persuasive messages upward or downward
   • Negative messages downward (usually)

2. *The circuitous pattern* should be used in messages where it is not strategically wise (or safe) to disclose your purpose forthrightly and immediately. Therefore, the circuitous pattern is appropriate in:

   • Negative messages upward (and sometimes downward)
   • Negative persuasive messages upward or downward

---

*\*Bottom-Line Business Writing,* John S. Fielden, Ronald E. Dulek, © 1984, Prentice-Hall, Inc.

- Blind persuasive messages
- Any type of upwardly sent messages where the writer has sensible reasons to fear being forthright.

The interaction of style, organization, power position, and type of message is simply too complex to remember accurately. Therefore, it was obvious that a device was needed to help busy writers determine before they write:

- Exactly what type of message it is they are writing and whether they are sending it up or down.
- Which organizational pattern is probably best to use in presenting that type of message.
- What style is most likely to be best suited to that message, the direction it is being sent, and the organizational pattern chosen.

What resulted is "The Wheel of Style," which is illustrated at the end of this book. Cut out the wheels, brad them together, and you have a handy summary of all the complex interactions that must be considered before you begin writing. All you need to do is to turn the dial to the type of message you must write and "The Wheel of Style" tells you which organizational pattern and which style of writing are most likely to produce the desired results from the reader.

## MINIMIZING YOUR STYLE RISKS

While we cannot guarantee success if you follow the generalizations about style and organizational pattern shown by "The Wheel of Style," we do assert emphatically that by giving serious consideration to the wheel's advice, you will be minimizing the risks you run in a given situation. If anything, the advice of "The Wheel of Style" is highly conservative—as it should be. But no mechanical device can take the place of your sound business judgment, based on your knowledge of the situation and the reader's relationship with you.

Only you know the types of people you regularly communicate with. Only you know the personality traits and idiosyncrasies of your particular customers and superiors. But bear in mind that the reactions of the businesspeople we tested to the predictions of "The Wheel of Style" were remarkably uniform. Hence, the style wheel does tell you the organizational pattern and style which nine times out of ten will prove effective. And that knowledge should certainly be helpful.

# HOW TO WRITE
# SUCCESSFUL MESSAGES
# TO EQUALS

A quick turn around "The Wheel of Style" reveals that messages being sent laterally, rather than up or down, are not included. This chapter tells why.

A great amount of business correspondence is carried on between people who are equals, or who at least have no direct power over each other. People communicate across functions or between departments in the same business organization. And people write in many instances to people outside their own organization who are neither up or down, but rather sideways.

Are there differences in the way such laterally sent messages should be organized? And are there stylistic differences also? Let's speculate as we have before.

First, it seems unlikely that—so long as the message content is not negative—there should be organizational and stylistic differences between up or down communications and laterally sent communications.

We have already seen that when a positive or a positive persuasive message is sent either up or down, it should always use a direct organization and a forceful, personal, and possibly even colorful style. We can think of no reason to suspect that such positive or positive persuasive messages should be differently engineered if they are sent from one peer to another.

Similarly, we can think of no reason why a laterally sent information-conveying message should differ from a similar message sent up or down. A quotation on the price of widgets is nothing more than a flat statement of the price, whether it is sent up, down, or sideways. In every instance, it can be forceful and personal, as appropriate, and probably colorless.

But what about negative and negative persuasive messages sent laterally across functions or departments or to nonpowerful outside organizations? Here there may be differences.

## SENDING NEGATIVE MESSAGES LATERALLY

In the business environment, it is not easy to conjure up many situations where one person is in a position to give bad news to a peer. In business, it seems to us that one of the equals has to be cast temporarily in the position of superior or subordinate in order for a negative message situation to occur. For instance, let's imagine that a colleague asks you to give her your opinion of a speech she is about to deliver, or a new product idea she has just dreamed up, a new package design, or an article she plans to submit to a professional journal. In each instance, she would temporarily place herself in a subordinate position to you and your judgment. So why should you not take heed of the conclusions we have come to about a negative message being sent down and write your review in a direct, somewhat forceful, impersonal, and colorless style?

But if we were to accept this conclusion we would be overlooking one important difference: tomorrow and for many days thereafter you will no longer be in that power position over her. And if you do not handle this temporary situation tactfully and sensitively, she may (in fact, she probably *will*) harbor significant resentments.

Let's imagine that Anne Siegal, a co-worker, has asked you to review a speech she has to deliver before a business group. You find that you do not like it. Because you don't want to risk losing her friendship, you decide to convey your negative opinion to her as if she were in the superior position. Therefore, you drop her the following note, organized circuitously and passive, impersonal, and colorless in style.

TO:  Anne

FROM: You

Thanks for giving me the opportunity to read the draft of your speech. It shows clearly how hard you have worked in gathering the detailed information you present. It is as intelligent and thorough a discussion of this topic as I have ever read.

It is possible, however, that some listeners may feel that it is too detailed for a luncheon talk. Its seriousness and in-depth treatment of the topic may possibly even be regarded as too intellectually demanding by some members of the audience.

Could it possibly be shortened and made less scholarly to suit the lighter expectations of a luncheon audience? Certainly, much of undoubted value would be sacrificed. On the other hand, greater audience receptivity might well be attained.

She reads this note and, while disappointed, is not offended by your approach. Yet she does wonder why—if you are such close friends—you chose such a circuitous organization and such a passive, impersonal style. In short, why are you so formal and distant?

However, since she is not stupid, she sees clearly that you really found her speech so boring and so far off the mark that you felt you had to draw back into formality and impersonality. The beating-around-the-bush organization, the weasel words, and attributing negative thoughts to faceless "others," she quickly senses, are your attempts to be tactful.

Now, suppose you wrote, instead, the following note, which is direct in organization and forceful, personal, and colorful in style.

TO:  Anne

FROM: You

Anne, for heaven's sake, don't give this speech. It's terrific, all right. It's certainly thorough, scholarly, and penetrating. But it's not right for a luncheon talk.

Send it in, as is, to *The Atlantic Monthly,* and put together a *Reader's Digest* version for the luncheon. As much as I like you, even I don't want to hear a doctoral thesis at lunch.

How would she react to this note? Frankly, we're not sure. On the one hand, she might *say* (and perhaps try to convince herself) that she appreciated your frankness. But would she, deep inside? We can't be sure.

While she would have recognized the artificiality of your approach in the first note, would she not also appreciate your desperate attempt not to offend?

And in the second note, would she possibly feel that you were *not* as considerate of her feelings and as tactful as a friend should be?

There is, as far as we can determine, no definite conclusion about which approach is best. Each of us has to make that decision; it is based on our individual relationship with our reader at that moment in time.

We recognize that you may be thinking, "I'd never *write* to a close friend in a situation like this." Well, that may indeed be true. But it makes no difference. Even if you go to give the bad news to your friend face to face, you still have to decide whether to be circuitous or direct, forceful or passive, personal or impersonal. Either way, in writing or face to face, *you* must make the decision. And remember, by writing you can control exactly what you say. You can't always do so when communicating orally. There are no erasers, unfortunately, on our tongues.

## DIRECTING NEGATIVE PERSUASIVE MESSAGES LATERALLY

In business, we very frequently find ourselves in situations where we must try to convince equals to do something they don't want to do, something against their personal best interests. Do we organize negative persuasive messages to equals the same way as we would such messages sent up or down? Do we use the same style?

"The Wheel of Style" reminds us that in negative persuasive messages sent both up and down, we use a circuitous organizational pattern. Does the same hold true when we are writing laterally to equals?

As for style, we have drawn a distinction between negative persuasive messages sent up and those sent down. For up, we decided to tend toward the passive, impersonal, and colorless. And for down, we decided to be somewhat forceful, but probably impersonal and colorless. What about when we are communicating laterally?

Let's experiment by inventing a situation where we are a member of a team of equals working on an important project. The next two weeks of teamwork on the project—July 15–29—are critical. You learn that one essential member of the team, Kathy Burns, has scheduled a vacation for the second week of this period, July 22–29. Her absence will make it impossible for the rest of the team to make progress.

She is currently working on a part of the project that causes her to be at a plant site in another town. Therefore, you resolve to write to her (rather than risk this delicate task to a telephone conversation where you can neither control exactly what you say nor see her face to get feedback as you would in a personal interview). Your task is to persuade her to change her vacation plans for the good of the other team members' ability to make progress on the project.

Here is the note you write.

TO:    Kathy Burns

FROM: You

I'm sorry to have to ask, but we need you to postpone your vacation plans for July 22–29.

You know how critical you are to our team efforts on this project. Without you, none of us—Joe, Bill, or Helen—can make any progress at all.

Obviously, when you made your vacation plans, you had no idea that they would coincide with this critical period on our project.

Please let us know your decision. We're counting on you, Kathy.

Now, here's a memo that is direct in organizational pattern, fairly forceful, and highly personal in style. In fact, it uses its personal statements to try to make Kathy feel guilty about handicapping her fellow team members. Would Kathy become angry because of the approach you have taken? Probably not.

But would this letter persuade her to defer her vacation plans? Again, probably not. Other than offering a little guilt manipulation, it is hardly persuasive. Can't Kathy easily conclude that the other team members are being selfish (they took their vacations, didn't they?) or exaggerating her importance to their effort?

Now, suppose you had concluded that Kathy is really in the driver's seat here. She is the superior (temporarily), and you are the beggar. What would a memo have looked like if it had followed the organizational pattern (circuitous) and style (passive, impersonal, and colorless) suggested for the negative persuasive communication upward? (In this case, since Kathy is not really a superior, you decide to be only somewhat passive and impersonal.) Here's what results:

TO:    Kathy Burns

FROM: You

It is believed imperative that our current project be completed by its August 31 deadline. This project, moreover, is a key element in the marketing plan being developed by the division for end-of-the-year presentation to corporate.

Of critical importance are the next two weeks of effort. From July 15–29 the team has been called upon to set criteria by which we will judge alternative product marketing strategies. A vital contribution thus is to be made by each team member.

The contributions made by you to the project have to date been outstanding. And continued contributions are actually critical during the July 15–29 period of criteria setting. In fact, the absence of such input will make it impossible for a balanced set of criteria to result from the rest of the team.

Therefore, despite full recognition of the fact that your vacation is richly deserved, we request that you postpone your vacation until after July 29. Your talents and expertise are critically needed during this two-week period. Please advise me of your decision as soon as possible.

How would this circuitous, passive, largely impersonal version go over with Kathy? Frankly, we don't think either version would prove effective if Kathy had purchased nonrefundable cruise tickets or if she felt that her fellow team members should have worked harder months ago so that the current crisis could have been avoided. And, perhaps above all, both versions reveal that the writer is in no position to offer any sort of carrot or bargaining chips. The sacrifice is all Kathy's.

## SOME EQUALS ARE MORE EQUAL

Furthermore, even the notion of equals raises a bewildering number of perplexing questions. Who really are equals in companies? For example, two employees have the same rank, but one has twenty years service and the other has one year. Are they equals? Does the employee with seniority have greater power? Or is he considered over the hill? Is the younger a mere rookie or is she "new blood" or a "young turk"?

Moreover, someone who is ostensibly an equal may be a friend of your boss or a protégé of someone important in your organization.

As a result, it seems impossible to set up case situations where we could test hypothetical responses as we have in the up and down situations. There it was easy. The boss or a big customer is a superior. A subordinate or a supplier is a subordinate. But who is an equal and how are equals defined? At the end of *Animal Farm,* George Orwell wrote, "All pigs are equal; only some pigs are more equal than others."

Our philosophical caveats about equals, however, only serve to point out that in real life, as opposed to hypothetical cases in a book such as this, you usually have a pretty good idea about whether or not the person you are writing to is one up on you, or vice versa. And if you do know, consult the style wheel for its advice. Then temper that advice with your personal knowledge of the reader and the situation.

## PERSUASION IS BARGAINING

Remember, too, that our attempts to persuade Kathy Burns to give up her vacation were predicted to fail, largely because the other team members gave up nothing while asking Kathy to give up everything. Under such circumstances, style alone can hardly be expected to perform miracles.

Suppose, however, that you realize this and try to strike a bargain with Kathy. Consider this approach:

TO:    Kathy Burns

FROM: You

Kathy, the other team members and I have decided to work through this and the next weekend so as to get our marketing plan criteria set before July 20 when your vacation is planned. In this way we will be able to keep making progress during your well-deserved vacation.

You have made so very many vital contributions to our project that we simply couldn't ask you to defer your vacation. But we did feel that we could ask you to work with us on the weekends, because we simply must have your input.

We'll meet in the small conference room at 10:00 on Saturday morning, and for the first weekend, at least, also work through Sunday.

Now, what do you think Kathy's reaction would be? Far more positive, we should think. And positive it should be, for you have magically changed the message from negative persuasive to positive persuasive. The message takes on a positive tone because it shows Kathy that her fellow team members are willing to inconvenience themselves to preserve her vacation schedule.

Since this message is now essentially positive, it can be direct, forceful, and personal. But is it persuasive as well? We think so. This message has a greater chance than the earlier versions of motivating Kathy to say, "Hey, gang, that's decent of you. But I can postpone my trip. And I really appreciate your concern." At the very worst, all of you will have to work two weekends, but even so, Kathy will think better of you and the group.

Style has made a difference, but only because some bargaining chips have been pushed Kathy's way.

Perhaps that is why negative persuasive messages sent laterally are so difficult. If people are truly equals, then it is difficult for the asker to be in a position to do something for the reader, to be able to make an offer he or she cannot refuse.

Success in such instances, we would think, will not result from organizational pattern or style used. It will result from the writer's ability to make an attractive offer.

# 18

## WHAT GIVES YOUR MESSAGES THEIR TONE?

Because tone is so difficult to define and discuss and because it is so closely intertwined with style, it seemed best in this book to defer consideration of tone until we had a clearer understanding of style. Now we are ready to deal with this difficult concept and to assess the relationship between style and tone.

*Tone* is a word that is frequently applied to written communications. We frequently hear statements like, "I don't like the tone of this letter; I don't like it at all." We hear people refer to a communication's "nasty" tone, its "whining" tone, its "mocking" tone, its "pleasant" tone, its "flat" tone, its tone of "high seriousness," or its tone of "self-importance." We know what all of these adjectives mean. But what is meant by the word *tone* itself?

We suspect the concept of tone is borrowed from oral communication, where it mostly refers to a person's tone of voice, the pitch or inflection employed by the speaker to add meaning beyond that carried by the actual words used. But can a piece of writing have a good or bad tone? Can a writer's tone of voice actually be heard by a reader? Probably not, but many readers think it can, and that's why they say, "I don't like this person's tone!" They are reading into the mesage some additional—usually emotional—meaning beyond that denoted specifically by the words themselves.

## DISTINGUISHING TONE FROM STYLE

How, then, does tone differ from "style," from the way something is said? Aren't they the same thing? The answer is yes and no. Style and tone might be considered as opposite sides of the same coin. A writer uses a given style and organizational pattern to convey a message. A reader may or may not react emotionally to what the writer has said and the way it is said. A tone is implied by a writer through the style he or she uses; and a tone is, for the most part, inferred by a reader through his or her emotional reaction to the writer's style. That is why we define tone as the capacity a given style has for producing an emotional reaction in the reader.

One of the reasons why writing is so difficult in a business situation is that the reader's reaction may actually be independent of both the content of the message and the style in which the message is delivered. You simply cannot always predict the mood or frame of mind that the reader will be in at the time of reading your communication.

If there are extenuating circumstances that have recently entered the life of the reader at home or at work, such as a fight with a spouse the previous evening or disappointment in his or her own performance at a staff conference just completed, that reader may have a negative reaction to any kind of communication delivered in any kind of style.

It is seldom easy to anticipate a reader's reaction. The reaction may come from inside the reader and then be projected onto the communication, often regardless of what the writer actually intended.

When the reader's reaction is largely independent of either the content of the message or the writer's style, you are absolutely helpless to improve the situation. This kind of problem with tone is therefore beyond the scope of this book.

The kind of problem with tone that we can profitably discuss is when the reader's reaction is likely to be largely dependent on both the content of the message and the style in which it is presented.

For example, we don't like it when we are told no in a situation in which we wanted a positive response. Our reaction stems mainly from the negative content of the message and to a lesser degree from the style of the message. But the impact of the negative content can be reduced if we 1) use an appropriate style of delivery, and 2) use an appropriate organizational pattern, direct or circuitous. We thereby can leave the reader with a less unfavorable reaction than he or she would have if we used the wrong style and organization.

The more negative the message, the more sensitive the reader is to its style. It's much easier to become upset when being told no than when being told yes, although it is possible to be told yes in such a begrudging, condescending, or nasty way that we react negatively to the style in spite of the positive content of the message. Thus, the writer must always be sensitive to style and must be especially sensitive when the communication conveys an unpleasant message.

In summary, then, tone problems usually occur in sensitive messages. Tone is the reader's reaction to what the writer says (the message), how the writer says it (the style), and when the writer chooses to get to a sensitive thought (the organizational pattern). The type of message is usually not within the writer's control (bad news is bad news), but how and when the writer delivers the message are. Also not within the writer's control are factors such as these:

- The reader's disposition in general.
- The reader's power position relative to the writer.
- The reader's opinion of the writer or of people in the writer's position.
- The immediate circumstances surrounding the reader's receipt of the message.
- The reader's mood when he or she gets the message.

## SEVEN SIMPLE WAYS TO MAKE READERS MAD

In addition to being sensitive to the reaction you may evoke in the reader by message, organization, and style, you must consider that readers may have special areas in which they are always sensitive and read in accusations or insults that the writer never intended, at least not consciously.

We have all received letters in which we feel the tone is so bad that we suspect it must have been intentional. Or perhaps the writer's deeper feelings have crept in without his or her actually being conscious of them and have affected a word choice or a turn of phrase that readers react to. Passive aggression doubtless often finds an outlet in a writer's style.

Sometimes it takes only a short phrase—or even a single word—to cause a reader to feel there is a bad tone, either consciously or not, in a message. For example:

1. Some readers react quite negatively to words and phrases that subtly imply they are liars:

   •"You claim that...."
   •"You state that...."
   •"According to you...."

2. Others become incensed at real or imaginary implications that they are stupid:

   •"As I've told you many times...."
   •"Even a child could understand...."

3. Many react negatively to perceived implications that they are merely gripers:

   •"We have received your complaint...."
   ("What?" says the reader. "I *never* complain.")

4. Readers are particularly sensitive, for some reason, about letter openings and closings. For example, take this letter opening:

   •"I was sorry to hear about your troubles with our product."
   ("Oh?" says the prickly reader. "You weren't sorry I had trouble; you were just sorry to *hear* about it.")

5. Letter closings are sensitive locations, too.
   Consider how this ending rakes up negative thoughts:

   •"I sincerely hope that these actions will compensate you adequately for all the problems you experienced with our product."

6. People are especially sensitive about their names, titles, and personal status:

   •*Mr.* to a woman.
   •*Mrs.* to a single woman.

•*Mr., Ms.,* or *Mrs.* to a *Dr.*

•*Dear Helen* or *Dear Bob* from a stranger.

7. Many readers are supersensitive about words associated with race relations, women's rights, age, and other personal attributes.

•*Girl.*

•*Boy.*

•*His* instead of *his or her.*

•*Identifying a person as black* or *female* when others are not identified as *white* or *male.*

Remember that the writer implies something with every word and phrase, while the reader may infer something entirely different from, or more or less than, what the reader intended to imply. As writers, all we can do is be cognizant of the fact that certain areas can be trouble spots for some readers. Therefore, we should avoid using words and phrases that have even a slight possibility of evoking a strongly negative reaction.

---

## POSITIVE TONE BUILDERS

Many words and phrases affect readers positively, usually because they show deference and cordiality on the part of the writer. Almost all polite words that bow to the reader's sensitivities fall into this category:

- "Please...."
- "Respectfully request...."
- "Sincerely regret...."
- "Sincerely apologize...."
- "If there is anything I can do...."
- "Thank you for...."

Words or phrases that praise readers and their efforts usually (unless blatantly overdone) cause readers to admire a message's tone.

# 19

## TONE PROBLEMS YOU FACE WHEN BEING FORCEFUL OR PASSIVE IN STYLE

In many situations, a reader's perception of the tone of a communication is almost completely dependent upon the style used. When this is the case, you can predict with reasonable accuracy the general capacity that each of your business styles has to produce the tone you want. Let's summarize what we have learned about the potential each style has for producing the desired tone. We'll begin by analyzing the possible reader problems you face by choosing to use either the forceful or the passive style.

### USE THE FORCEFUL STYLE JUDICIOUSLY

A forceful style imparts to readers a feeling that the writer is in command, self-assured, direct, and forthright, and personally responsible for what is being said.

Aren't all of these qualities desirable in a writer? Not necessarily. We've learned that it depends upon the content of the message and the relative positions of the writer and the reader. There are times when being forceful is the only way to get the job done. But there are also times when being forceful is tantamount to being suicidal.

If a writer is reporting how he or she fouled up, being forthright and taking personal responsibility may not be a bit smart. Nor do you want to write to your boss, saying, "Your decision to close the plant in August is not only stupid but will result in dire consequences." Obviously, these are times when a passive style is appropriate. If the content of the message is purely factual and the facts are of relatively little importance to the reader, a passive style or a style halfway between passive and forceful may also be appropriate.

But, by definition, all generalizations are only generally true. There are times when you may really want to write upward in a forceful style and are willing to pay the price if a superior resents your tone—actually your forceful style. If so, do so. But we, or any other teachers of writing, can hardly recommend this as a general practice.

Employing a passive style when the writer seeks to impress or even intimidate the reader will usually cause tone problems. The reader may not actually say, "I don't like the tone of this message." But the reader may react psychologically to the perceived limpness and passivity of the style. Striking a balance between looking wishy-washy when writing a message down (especially a negative message) and appearing overbearing is not always easy.

---

## BLENDING THE FORCEFUL AND PASSIVE STYLES

When in doubt, the skilled writer may use a mixture of forceful and passive statements and walk the fine line between perceived weakness and dictatorialness. Let's consider how we might make the following message seem less overbearing:

> I have decided not to continue funding your project. Cease all further efforts, and prepare a thorough report on what benefits have been realized to date on this project.

We could put everything into the passive and in the process eliminate the imperatives *cease* and *prepare*.

A decision has been made to discontinue funding your project. All further efforts should cease. A thorough report on what benefits have been realized to date should be prepared.

We'll assume that the writer of this memo is highly sensitive and experienced. While he did not like the implication of overbearing egotism in the forceful version, he recognizes that the passive version may not serve his purpose as well either. By saying, "A decision has been made," the writer has been hidden away. And our experienced writer knows that he will lose face by not admitting his responsibility. "A decision has been made?" the angry reader thinks. "Phooey! You made it and haven't got the guts to tell me to my face."

Our writer is too smart to fall into this trap. He learned long ago that when the boss too obviously hides out, he or she is diminished in the eyes of subordinates. He remembers receiving a memo years ago that began, "Headquarters has decided against your proposal." "Headquarters has?" he thought. "Headquarters can't decide anything! *Who* didn't have the courage to own up to this decision?" That's what the reader of the message he is preparing now would undoubtedly think about the first sentence of the passive draft.

Our writer now seeks a compromise to express his first sentence. He realizes that the sentence, "A decision has been made to discontinue funding your project," is not only passive but also impersonal (who has made the decision?). One alternative is to put the person who has made the decision back into the sentence but still keep it passive. Thus, the sentence would read, "A decision has been made by me to discontinue funding your project."

The writer considers this version. He notes some softening of impact as a result of the passive voice. And he does see that he is somewhat obliquely accepting responsibility. But he suspects that this sentence, because of its passivity, may also damage his authority in the eyes of the reader.

Now he makes his final decision. He will be forceful in the first sentence, to own up to his personal responsibility. But he will immediately shift to the passive thereafter and eliminate the imperatives. Here's how the message would look:

I have decided not to continue funding your project. All further efforts should cease.

A thorough report on what benefits have been realized to date should be prepared.

Obviously, the reader will be unhappy with the message. But our writer feels satisfied in having engineered the exact tone he wanted by mixing forceful and passive statements that average out to make the total message neither too weak nor too forceful.

# 20

## TONE PROBLEMS YOU FACE WHEN BEING PERSONAL OR IMPERSONAL IN STYLE

A personal style of writing is warmly received by readers when a pleasant or positive message is being conveyed. People sometimes worry about the overuse of the pronoun *I*. There is nothing wrong with using *I* when you are saying pleasantries or giving a compliment such as, "I want to congratulate you on a job well done."

People generally seem to like the pronoun *you*. But, again, readers like *you* better when it is part of a positive message. "You have done a wonderful job," sounds just great.

But the use of personal pronouns—especially *you* and *I*—becomes highly questionable when you are conveying a negative or critical message. Statements like, "I think you have done a terrible job," or, "Your work is simply unsatisfactory," almost always evoke a negative reaction. In situations like these, making the negative comment personal increases the reader impact and heightens the possibility of a negative reaction to a message's perceived tone.

The same is true about being personal by using people's names in a negative situation. If you say, "Bill James caused this mistake to be made," James has the finger pointed directly at him. James himself undoubtedly would prefer an impersonal statement such as "The data processing director assumed responsibility for the error," or a completely passive statement like, "A mistake was made."

Similarly, a style that is personal because it is conversational may be appropriate in some situations and completely inappropriate in others. Some people like chatty messages. Others react negatively and dismiss the communication as too breezy in tone or one the writer felt was of so little importance that it could be dashed off.

When we recommend being impersonal in negative situations, we are not ruling out personal statements expressing care and concern about the reader as a person. But here is an area where the risk of equivocation is great—we may find ourselves mixing up two different meanings of *personal*.

Let's firmly keep in mind the fact that we have been talking about a personal style of writing that refers to such things as using personal pronouns, names of people, first names, questions, short sentences similar to ordinary conversation. An impersonal writing style does not in itself rule out the use of statements expressing care and concern about the reader. But such statements of caring can obviously be expressed in an impersonal as well as a personal style.

---

### EXAMPLE: NEGATIVE MESSAGE, PERSONAL STYLE, CIRCUITOUS PATTERN

This distinction is sometimes a bit hard to grasp. So let's take up a case and see what we can learn. Let's conjure up one of the most negative situations of all—a letter severing the reader from his or her job. We will write this highly negative message in a personal style, use the appropriate circuitous organizational pattern, and make every effort to express great personal care and concern about the reader:

Dear Robert:

No one realizes more than I do the tremendous amount of time and effort you put into attempting to make the Vulcan project viable. All of us in the company sincerely hoped that this project would prove successful and that matters would work out differently from the way they have.

Even though we have the greatest respect for your energy and dedication, I have the unfortunate responsibility to inform you that the project will be discontinued by the end of the year, and that there will be no further need of your services.

Let me assure you, Robert, that we regret this decision, no one more than I. You can be sure that we will give you the highest of personal recommendations and will do everything in our power to help you relocate. We sincerely regret that we have to take this action. And we regret the personal disappointment and inconvenience it causes you and your family.

This is really a very good letter. But the question is, would the letter be better received if it were less personal in style? Let's focus on some of the personal statements and then reduce the personal qualities in the style of each. Then we will put the letter back together and consider which version is better.

| | |
|---|---|
| *Original:* | "No one realizes more than I the tremendous amount of time and effort you put into...." |
| *Revised:* | "The tremendous amount of time and effort you put into attempting to make the Vulcan project viable is widely recognized." |
| *Original:* | "All of us in the company sincerely...." |
| *Revised:* | "It was sincerely hoped that this project...." |
| *Original:* | "Even though we have the greatest respect for your energy and...." |
| *Revised:* | "While there is the greatest respect for your energy...." |
| *Original:* | "I have the unfortunate responsibility to inform you that the project will be discontinued...." |
| *Revised:* | "The decision has been made to discontinue the project...." |
| *Original:* | "Let me assure you, Robert, that we regret this decision, no one more than I." |
| *Revised:* | "This decision is unfortunate." |
| *Original:* | "You can be sure that we will give you the highest of personal recommendations...." |
| *Revised:* | "The highest of personal recommendations will be gladly given...." |
| *Original:* | "...and we will do everything in our power to help relocate you." |
| *Revised:* | "...and everything possible will be done to facilitate your relocation." |
| *Original:* | "We sincerely regret that we have to take this action." |
| *Revised:* | (This sentence would be deleted.) |

*Original:*    "And we regret the personal disappointment and inconvenience it causes you and your family."

*Revised:*    (This sentence would be deleted.)

---

## REVISION: NEGATIVE MESSAGE, IMPERSONAL STYLE

The revised and far more impersonal letter, as far as style is concerned would read like this:

Dear Robert:

The tremendous amount of time and effort you put into attempting to make the Vulcan project viable is widely recognized. It was sincerely hoped that this project would prove successful and that matters would have turned out differently from the way they have.

While there is the greatest respect for your energy and dedication, the decision has been made to discontinue the project by the end of the year, and that there will be no further need of your services.

This decision is unfortunate. The highest of personal recommendations will be gladly given, and everything possible will be done to facilitate your relocation.

Whether the revised impersonal letter strikes you as superior to the personal first version or not, we have no way of knowing. All we can do is to offer our speculations for you to take into consideration and, as before, you accept what you agree with and reject what you don't.

It is only fair that we try our best to put ourselves in the position of Robert, who has just found his pet project discontinued and himself without a job. He is sitting in his office reading the first version of the letter. We have to ask ourselves not only how the warm personal observations in this original draft are going to be regarded by Robert, but whether they will continue to be so regarded after a second or third reading. That's the acid test.

---

## EXAMINING THE REACTION OF THE RECIPIENT

Let's look over the personal statements in the first draft and speculate how Robert might react to them. Assume that Robert has completed reading the letter for the first time, is stunned by the negative message he has received, and now is rereading the letter in a state of great disappointment, embarrassment, and chagrin.

If there ever were a time when a reader would be likely to read bad tone into a communication, this would be a classic instance. Let's speculate about how Robert's mind might operate:

"No one realizes more than I do...." If he realized how hard I worked, why did he turn against me and cancel the project?

"All of us in the company sincerely hoped...." Hopes aren't good enough. I needed support and funding, not hopes.

"Even though we had the greatest respect for your energy and dedication, I have the unfortunate responsibility...." This is certainly a great way of showing respect for how hard I worked. "Unfortunate responsibility" be darned. If he really felt so sad about it, he should have fought harder for the project and my job! Crocodile tears!

"Let me assure you, Robert, that we regret this decision, no one more than I." More crocodile tears. If he regretted it so much, why did he fire me? I'll never understand it.

"You can be sure that we will give you the highest of personal recommendations and we will do everything in our power to help you relocate." They don't even offer any hope of my staying with the company and perhaps taking on another project. This shows how insincere they are about all these expressions of great personal regret.

"We sincerely regret that we have to take this action." I guess they think if they keep saying that over and over again, I might get to believe it. But I won't!

"And we regret the personal disappointment and inconvenience it causes you and your family." Oh, my God, I've only been thinking of myself. What a blow this is going to be to Mary. And what about the kids in school? It means moving and financial problems. Despite all their pious expressions of warm personal regret, they don't care a hang about me, my family, or all the hard work I've put in.

Isn't that quite possibly just the way Robert would react in the situation we have set up? Let's take a second look at the revised impersonal version, which, literally speaking, is by no means as seemingly warm and caring a document as the first letter. But as you reread the second version, speculate about what effect its impersonality might have on Robert.

Again, he sits and reads through the letter once; then he reads it again. Naturally, Robert is just as shocked and disappointed as he was when he received the first letter. But he might not have the feeling that someone is trying to con him. What he has read is a flat, businesslike letter relating a business decision in a businesslike way. It leaves Robert as an individual out of the situation. It does not drag his wife and family into the picture. It doesn't shed what Robert was quick to characterize as crocodile tears.

## IMPERSONAL STYLE BETTER SUITS NEGATIVE MESSAGES DOWN

So what can we conclude? When writing negative messages down, it may often be wise to express warm and caring thoughts in a somewhat impersonal style. Expressing those warm thoughts in a personal style runs the risk of seeming phony and artificial.

Remember, we are talking about style only. We have never said that the writer cannot express personal comments that imply understanding and empathy with the reader, even though a negative decision is being conveyed. We are saying that these personal comments implying understanding and empathy probably should be written in an impersonal style.

You will notice that our revised letter conveyed exactly the same comments as the original. It expressed a recognition of how hard he had worked. It stated that it was hoped that the project would have proved successful and that things would have turned out differently, and that there still is the greatest respect for his energy and dedication. And it expressed recognition that this decision was unfortunate, certainly from Robert's point of view. It showed concern for his need for a recommendation and his need to relocate. But it expressed all these thoughts in an impersonal style, and that impersonal style may have kept Robert from feeling that everyone in the upper reaches of the company was looking at him and shaking their heads in disappointment over his failure.

There is no denying that the revised version is colder and more businesslike. It is possible that the coldness of this version would also be resented by Robert. It is also possible that there is no way that one can ruin, even temporarily, someone's life and have that person like the letter that conveys the bad news.

Our conclusion is that many a crocodile tear has been shed by businesspeople when they write negative messages downward, beating their breasts and wiping their eyes. To do so, however, may expose the writer to the risk of being accused of expressing phony personal feelings.

But you, in your own job, have to take this discussion and carry it in mind the next time you have to write a difficult letter like this one. It could be that some combination of both versions might be even more acceptable to Robert than either of our previous versions. There is no way we can be absolutely sure.

# 21

## TONE PROBLEMS YOU FACE WHEN BEING COLORFUL OR COLORLESS IN STYLE

Including adjectives and adverbs in a message clearly increases its impact on the reader. But there is no way to judge outside of a given situation whether that impact is going to be beneficial or harmful. Colorful writing shows up all the time in advertisements and other marketing situations, but the same style frequently jars in other types of business writing—particularly those of a more scientific or technical nature.

Most business writing is, in fact, almost completely colorless. It seldom contains figures of speech and usually has very few adjectives and adverbs other than the standard business buzz words and phrases like "exciting new opportunities," "expanding vistas," "sharpening our growing edge," and other sanctified chestnuts. In most business writing, the colorful language of advertising and marketing would stick out like a sore thumb (to use a simile and a cliché). You must use common sense in the application of colorful language to your writing, as with each of the other styles, in order to reduce the possibility of a negative reaction because of the perceived tone.

Our experiments have repeatedly shown that highly colorful writing almost always produces in the reader a tone of amused derision or embarrassment. We apparently can put up with fulsome writing in advertisements and direct mail messages. And, as readers, we don't care much about what style positive messages are conveyed in. But when colorful writing is personally directed to us, especially in negative, negative pesuasive, and information-conveying situations, we find ourselves either annoyed or amused, or both!

Let's invent a situation in which colorful writing might very well be appropriate. Suppose we have to write a congratulatory letter to be read by our manager at a retirement dinner being given for a vice-president. If there ever was a time when a few colorful phrases might be appropriate, this is it. Here's the colorful draft we come up with:

Dear Henry,

Congratulating you on your well-earned retirement is as completely inadequate as congratulating Sam Snead for his decades of championship-level golf.

Like Snead to duffers, you have been a positive inspiration to all of us in sales. You've shown that championship-level selling can continue year after year—if we'd only try as hard as you.

It's been an absolute joy to all of us going out to the sales wars shoulder to shoulder with you. No one will ever take your place in our sincere devotion, our deepest respect, and our eternal memories.

Everyone in the function joins me in wishing you the ultimate in joy and happiness for many years ahead.

We have created an excellent version of a colorful letter. No attempt has been made to burlesque the style. Yet, when our manager sees this draft, he or she is very likely to say, "I can't take this to my boss to sign. He'll laugh at it. He'd never sign something like this!"

"What's wrong with it?" you ask.

"I don't know. It sounds too gushy, I guess. It's just too much. Tone it down a little. No, tone it down a lot!" (*Tone* it down! Reduce the emotional impact this draft might have on an audience.)

## COLORFUL STYLE EASILY INVITES EXCESS

Why would somone possibly—or, more likely, probably—react so negatively to this draft? Most people would not have the vocabulary to express why they perceive an objectionable tone to this fine letter. But we know.

First of all, it uses poetic figures of speech:

- "Congratulating you on your well-earned retirement is as inadequate as congratulating Sam Snead...." (This is a simile: A is like B.)
- "Like Snead to duffers, you...." (This is another simile.)
- "Duffers" is itself a metaphor. Ordinary salespeople are to Henry as a duffer is to Snead.
- "Going out to the sales wars" (This is a metaphor—selling is war.)
- "Shoulder to shoulder" is a metaphor. We are not literally fighting shoulder to shoulder as soldiers would.

Second, it employs many adjectives and adverbs:

- "well-earned"
- "completely inadequate"
- "championship-level"
- "absolute"
- "positive"
- "sincere"
- "deepest"
- "eternal"
- "ultimate"
- "many"

Third, it engages in hyperbolic exaggerations (hyperbole, exaggeration for special effect, is another poetic figure of speech).

- "Absolute joy." Probably nothing is really absolute. In particular, working with someone certainly wouldn't rank with many other joys that come to mind.
- "A positive inspiration." Inspiration connotes almost a religious or mystical association.

- "Our sincere devotion, our deepest respect, and our eternal memories." Again, it could well sound as if one is referring to a saint or a fallen national hero.

All in all, this analysis shows clearly that:

1. Your manager won't take it to her boss.
2. If she did, the boss probably wouldn't sign it.
3. If it had actually been read at the retirement party, somebody might have giggled, or more likely Henry might have squirmed in embarrassment.

What conclusion is fair to draw? Should we never use any colorful expressions? Our personal opinion is that a colorful style should be used sparingly in almost every writing situation other than the supposedly seductive advertisement and the highly positive message. It is often impossible to praise some people too highly or in too flowery a style. For the rest of your communications, use a colorful style only in sentences sprinkled sparingly (to be colorful about it) like delicate spices.

# HOW TO ENGINEER YOUR STYLE AND ORGANIZATIONAL PATTERN TO ACHIEVE DESIRED RESULTS

Style and organizational pattern do interrelate in their effect on a reader. As figures 22–1 and 22–2 show, styles can be chosen either to augment or to counteract the impact an organizational pattern has on a reader.

A directly organized letter (schematically represented in figure 22-1) gets right to the point in the first paragraph. Bang! If the author writes in a forceful, personal, or even a colorful style (as shown by the arrows at the bottom of figure 22-1), the already high impact of this letter will be greatly increased. If the writer decides that the subject matter is too sensitive to be presented in such a high-impact fashion, he or she can consider changing the style used, making it more passive, impersonal or colorless (as shown by the arrows at the top of figure 22-1) so as to lower the letter's total impact.

Perhaps, as figure 22-2 shows, the writer concludes that it is unwise in this case to use such a direct organizational pattern, and decides to be circuitous. Now the point of this sensitive message only comes to light in the last paragraph, after much

Tone
Counter-acting
Styles

Using passive, impersonal,
or colorless style with a
direct pattern, softens the
impact the direct pattern
has on a reader.

Using a forceful, personal,
or colorful style with a
direct organizational pattern increases the impact
the direct pattern has on a
reader.

Tone
Augmenting
Styles

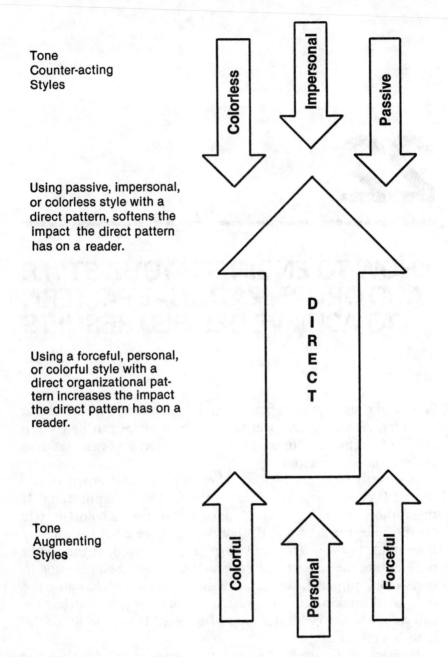

FIGURE 22–1. Synergistic and Countersynergistic Effects of Style and
Organizational Pattern on Tone.

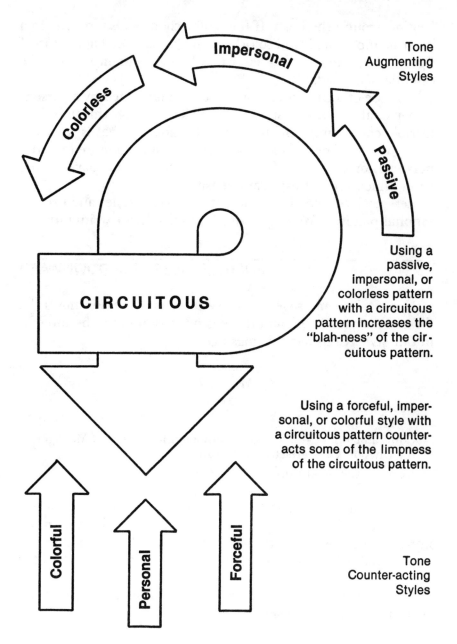

Tone
Augmenting
Styles

Using a
passive,
impersonal, or
colorless pattern
with a circuitous
pattern increases the
"blah-ness" of the cir-
cuitous pattern.

Using a forceful, imper-
sonal, or colorful style with
a circuitous pattern counteracts some of the limpness
of the circuitous pattern.

Tone
Counter-acting
Styles

FIGURE 22–2.

beating around the bush. If the writer chooses also to write in a passive, impersonal, and colorless style (as indicated at the top of figure 22-2), the resulting letter may be so low in impact as to be essentially unreadable.

The use of a circuitous organization, augmented by a passive, impersonal, colorless style, will make wading through it a terrible chore, even for the hardiest reader. If that is what the writer wants—fine. If not, he or she can opt for a more forceful, personal, or even colorful style—at least in those parts of the letter which are not especially sensitive.

Let's try a couple of experiments in mixing styles and organizational patterns. We begin with a positive letter written down.

## POSITIVE MESSAGES DOWNWARD

In a positive message, we know there is no reason not to be direct in organization, and there is no reason not to be forceful in our style. Consider this message:

*Version I*

Dear Joan:

Congratulations! You are to be promoted to Personnel Manager for Division One, effective this February 15.
Keep up the good work!

Clearly, the forceful style and the direct organization complement each other and give this positive message even more impact. There is no possibility that the way the promotion was announced will seem begrudging or halfhearted in tone to the reader.

Now let's write the same letter in the same direct organization pattern, but in a passive style:

*Version II*

Dear Joan,

A promotion to Personnel Manager, effective Feburary 15, has been approved for you.
It is anticipated that the good work will be kept up by you.

What are the tone implications of this second version? Joan may actually resent the coldness of this version. And because of the passive voice's penchant for burying the subject, it is not at all clear to Joan that the writer is actually happy about her promotion.

Now let's try a version of this letter that mixes a forceful style with a circuitous organizational pattern:

*Version III*

Dear Joan,

We have thoroughly screened all internal personnel whose qualifications and experience serve to make them candidates for the position of Personnel Manager. There were many outstanding candidates.

Your qualifications are excellent and your experience more than sufficient. I assure you that every factor in your favor was considered.

For these reasons, I am delighted to inform you that you are to be promoted to Personnel Manager for Division One, effective February 15. Congratulations!

What will be Joan's reaction to this third version? Don't you think the delay in giving the good news will negatively affect the way Joan will react to the letter? We think so, regardless of the forcefulness of the style employed. In fact, the circuitous organizational pattern completely counteracts the impact of the forceful style. Version III might be useful if we really didn't want Joan to be promoted and wanted her to know it.

What's our conclusion? Unless there are reasons not to do so, we should use the style that complements the organizational pattern used. For letters in the direct pattern, be forceful. For letters written in the circuitous pattern, be passive.

## NEGATIVE MESSAGES DOWNWARD

Let's examine another situation illustrating the effect that the interrelationship of style and organization has on tone. We'll use as an example an actual form letter sent out by a large company to reject college graduates who have interviewed for jobs:

Mr. Randy Davis
123 Main Street
Anytown, U.S.A.

Dear Mr. Davis:

Thank you for taking the time to interview with our recruiter on your campus.

We have processed your application. Your qualifications, unfortunately, were not equal to those of other applicants.

Therefore, we can offer you no encouragement about possible employment with ABCD.

We appreciate your interest in ABCD.

Sincerely,

The writer of this letter has used the bare bones of the circuitous pattern plus a forceful style:

- The first sentence–paragraph says something nice but does not contain the point of the communication, which is to say no. But the brevity of this paragraph doesn't buffer the twin hammer blows that follow immediately.
- "We have processed your application" is hardly a pleasantry. Davis may feel that his application went through a machine, like a sausage. Then, the second paragraph tells him that his qualifications were not equal to those of others. This is gratuitously insulting. The young man asked for a job, not a disparagement of his relative qualifications.
- The third paragraph tells him no.
- The last paragraph is an attempt to be civil but is largely a rubber-stamp expression meaning nothing.

Why might Davis react unfavorably to this letter? Why wouldn't he like its tone? Doesn't it follow the time-honored "bury the negative" circuitous organizational pattern appropriate to the no-letter?

Sure, but the forceful style wars with the indirect organizational pattern. Its crisp, simple, subject–verb–object active voice sentences and its short punchy paragraphs all rain powerful psychological blows on the reader.

Would a better letter have resulted if a passive style more suited to this letter's circuitous pattern had been used? Let's see:

Dear Mr. Davis:

The time you spent interviewing on campus was much
appreciated. Through such an in-depth interview, an opportunity
to learn more about your career goals and interests was obtained.

The application you sent us has been reviewed with great interest,
as were, of course, the applications of the many other fine
graduates who, like you, interviewed with ABCD.

As you learned during the interview, few openings are available at
this time. And for each of these openings there were literally an
overwhelming number of applicants. Therefore, many strong
candidates such as yourself cannot be encouraged.

We thank you, however, for giving us the chance to talk with you.
And we wish you success in your future career.

Obviously the passive style better complements the circuitous
pattern, and most probably would be better received by Davis
than would the first version.

---

## EXCEPTIONS TO THE RULE

Must we be doctrinaire in our use of style and organizational
pattern? Should we never mix direct organizations and passive
style, or circuitous organization and forceful style?

Of course, you can do anything you want. But whatever you
do should be for sound reasons. For example:

1. You have to write a negative message upward in your organization. You know that you should be circuitous in organizational
   pattern and passive, impersonal, and colorless in style. But the
   combination of circuitous pattern and passive style seems cow-
   ardly to you because this issue is something you feel strongly
   about, and you want to stand up and be counted. You decide,
   therefore, to construct two drafts, one combining a forceful style
   with a circuitous pattern and the other a passive, impersonal style
   with a direct organizational pattern. You will select the draft that
   adequately displays your courage and integrity but reduces the
   risk of causing resentment (and resistance) on the part of your
   superiors.

2. You need to write a positive letter down, but you question whether
   the reader will take the good news as a license not to work as hard.
   You are leery, therefore, of being too personally congratulatory.
   You decide to write a memo that offers congratulations directly
   but is throttled back severely in terms of personal and forceful
   qualities. You hope that your reserved tone may keep the reader
   on his or her toes.

# PUTTING YOUR KNOWLEDGE TO WORK ON A TOUGH CASE

We have learned much in our experimenting and thinking together. But can we capture and put to use what we have learned? Is our knowledge simply a collection of theories that lack practical application? Let's find out by applying this knowledge to a difficult communications case.

### Case

The new vice-president for materials management of a large multiplant corporation is faced with writing a letter to the company's seven purchasing managers located around the nation. He has spoken with them by phone and indicated that he has before the board of directors a proposal for making immediate changes in purchasing procedures. He promised to write them to outline these changed procedures upon board approval.

This is the first letter he has written to them. The message involves telling them of changes in procedures that will decrease the autonomy of local purchasing managers. Naturally, he wants this change to take place with a minimum of negative damage to morale. Yet, on the other hand, he does not wish to appear weak or indecisive in this letter, because he knows that the purchasing managers will be sizing him up.

He has decided against a face-to-face meeting with these managers—either individually or as a group—because he does not wish to get into a public argument over this needed change. He realizes there is no way he can persuade the local managers that centralized control will do anything but impede their efforts to obtain needed materials for their local plants. What he does hope to accomplish is to minimize the message's potential for making the local managers feel personally demoted.

Consider the facts of the case in light of what you now know about the interaction of type of message, style, and organizational pattern. Begin by analyzing the type of message we are dealing with:

1. The message is negative (as readers will undoubtedly perceive it).
2. However, we want to try (at least) to persuade the readers that the changes in procedures are for the good of the corporation.
3. And we are writing down. We are playing the role of the vice-president, who is the readers' superior officer.
4. Therefore, we conclude that we must write a negative persuasive message downward.

Dial "negative persuasive message downward" on "The Wheel of Style," and see that such a message, to have the best chance (not the *only* chance) of being at least minimally well received by the reader, should be:

1. Circuitously organized.
2. Written in a style that is:
   • Somewhat forceful.
   • Probably impersonal.
   • Probably colorless.

Notice all the qualifiers—somewhat, probably, probably. This is because all negative situations are so touchy that flat-footed generalizations are dangerous. "The Wheel of Style" has merely pointed us in what is probably the right direction. It is for us to decide whether a given situation with a particular reader calls for us to use a style that is more forceful than somewhat, or more definitely impersonal than probably so, and definitely colorless rather than probably colorless.

## THE WHEEL POINTS THE WAY

"The Wheel of Style" has already proved its value, because most of us—if we had followed our emotional instincts—might have fired off a memo like this:

TO:     Plant Purchasing Managers

FROM: Vice-President, Materials Management

I have today received approval from the board of directors for a change in our purchasing procedures. As a result, you and other purchasing managers in each plant must notify me about any contracts you are negotiating in excess of $25,000. I must receive your notification at least two weeks before you sign such contracts. You may not actually sign any contract unless you receive written permission from me.

I expect your complete cooperation in supporting my attempts to bring coördination into our corporationwide purchasing activities. Details of these procedural changes are attached.

Clearly, a memo of this type would have flown in the face of the advice given by "The Wheel of Style." It is direct rather than circuitous; it is extremely forceful and very personal in style, the combination ending up in a stream of imperatives ("you must notify me," "I must receive," "I expect your complete cooperation") that might do justice to Captain Bligh. The personal nature of the draft can be seen in the fact that fifteen of its ninety-two words are personal pronouns.

Our experiments have pointedly indicated that being personal in a negative situation usually serves only to heighten the negative quality of the message. The personal style of this memo essentially points the finger at each individual reader and says, "you'd better do as I say." The combination of a forceful, personal style with a direct organizational pattern makes this memo seem far too overbearing, even bullying. We are glad the vice-president did not send out such a disastrous memo.

We resolve to go in the direction recommended by "The Wheel of Style" and focus on the fact that we are writing a negative persuasive memo downward. The vice-president is not just conveying bad news; he is trying to persuade undoubtedly unwilling readers to accept not only the changed procedures, but him as their leader.

We will make an attempt to sell the change in policy as something positive for the company—and hence for the purchasing managers. Such an approach obviously calls for a circuitous organizational pattern. A circuitous approach will call for him to be less forceful in style. Negative messages are best delivered more impersonally than personally. Here is how a beginning paragraph written along these lines might look:

> As a vital part of our company's far-flung purchasing actvities, you will want and need to know about a significant change in our purchasing procedures just approved by the board of directors. Starting immediately, there will be a closer working relationship between your office and mine. Here is how we will work together to coordinate our corporate materials requirements, to insure the flow of materials to plants in greatest need, and to minimize prices paid.

Does the use of the circuitous pattern to front-end load a number of compliments run a significant risk of conveying a tone of artificiality, even insincerity, to hostile readers? How will such readers react to phrases like these?

- "As vital parts of your company's far-flung purchasing activities." Will readers think the colorful adjectives "vital" and "far-flung" smack of overwriting or, frankly, hogwash?
- "We will work together" (We will? That's what you think!)

---

### THE READER'S REACTION IS PARAMOUNT

This first paragraph deserves the wastebasket, but the notion of trying to state as much of the message as possible in terms of readers' interests continues to be an idea not easily cast aside. It is clear that artificiality and insincerity are the greatest risks in writing this letter to hostile subordinates. Trying to "con" them into thinking that these wing-clipping changes are all for their own good is not only impossible but probably a highly foolish attempt.

Therefore, the vice-president resolves to try a new beginning, one that very frankly but moderately impersonally admits to the conflict between central administration's desires and local administration's wishes. However, in this draft, he decides to increase the forcefulness of his style:

> An essential part of our new working relationship will be frank and open communication. Since my office's interests are long-

range and companywide while yours focus on the immediate needs of your location, we will inevitably at times appear to be at cross purposes.

The subject of this memo, which is to announce a significant change in corporate purchasing procedures, illustrates just such an occasion. Nevertheless, I expect you to appreciate why I have felt it necessary to recommend to the board of directors, and receive approval for, these changes.

These two opening paragraphs are good, still circuitous but not blatantly so. There is no obvious attempt made to flatter or "con" the purchasing managers.

The style is only somewhat impersonal. It uses *my* and *your* instead of *I* and *you,* and the style becomes increasingly impersonal as the subject veers toward the negative. The style never reaches the point of sounding as impersonal as a textbook.

Suddenly, in the last sentence, the style changes and becomes more forceful and personal. Here the vice-president decides to stand up and be counted. He forcefully and personally lets the purchasing managers know what he expects of them. However, he has not ended up sounding like Captain Bligh, as might have happened earlier.

## TRYING A STYLE SWITCH

Now question whether he should continue in the strongly candid, forceful, personal style of the last sentence, or whether he should back off a bit on both the forcefulness and personal qualities of his style up to this point. Let's experiment. First, consider a third paragraph that is quite passive and impersonal:

Approval has been given for the following changes in purchasing procedures:

1. The office of Vice-President for Materials Management must be notified of any contracts in excess of $25,000.
2. Such notifications must be received at least two weeks before any contemplated contract signing.
3. No contracts may be signed without prior written permission from this office.

Needed coordination of our corporationwide purchasing activities is essential. Cooperation with this change is expected. Details of changes are attached.

This paragraph certainly is impersonal. The use of the passive has eliminated all personal pronouns. He even refers to himself as "the office of the Vice-President for Materials Management."

---

## RESUMPTION OF PREVIOUS STYLE

But how does this style make him appear in the eyes of the purchasing managers? Does it make him appear as if he is hiding behind passive, impersonal policy-manual types of statements? This style certainly does not suggest a human being talking with valued colleagues. Therefore, we reject this approach and decide to continue in the somewhat impersonal but forceful style of the first two paragraphs. He will talk with his subordinates, and he will be forceful but not overbearing:

> Starting immediately, there will be a closer working relationship between your office and mine. Here is how we will work together to coordinate our corporate materials requirement, to insure the flow of materials to plants in greatest need, and to minimize prices paid:
>
> 1. The office of the Vice-President for Materials Management must be notified about any contracts in excess of $25,000.
> 2. Such notification must be received at least two weeks before any contemplated contract signing.
> 3. No contracts may be signed without prior written permission from this office.
>
> All of you will, I know, want to cooperate to the fullest. Details of the new procedure are attached.

Now let's put the whole letter together and see what it looks like:

TO: Purchasing Managers
FROM: Vice-President of Materials Management

> An essential part of our new working relationship will be frank and open communication. Since my office's interests are long-range and companywide while yours focus on the immediate needs of your location, we will inevitably at times appear to be at cross purposes.
>
> The subject of this memo, which is to announce significant changes in corporate purchasing procedures, illustrates just such an occasion. Nevertheless, I expect you to appreciate why I have felt it necessary to recommend to the board of directors, and receive approval for, these changes.
>
> Starting immediately, there will be a closer working relationship between your office and mine. Here is how we will work together

to coordinate our corporate materials requirement, to insure the flow of materials to plants in greatest need, and to minimize prices paid:

1. The Office of the Vice-President for Materials Management must be notified about any contracts in excess of $25,000.
2. Such notifications must be received at least two weeks before any contemplated contract signing.
3. No contracts may be signed without prior written permission from this office.

All of you will, I know, want to cooperate to the fullest. Details of the new procedure are attached.

## ENGINEERED BUSINESS WRITING

This final draft does seem to be honest and candid. It uses a circuitous pattern to blunt the forcefulness of the way things are being said, by controlling when the negative information is presented. It is forceful and personal only in those parts of the letter where the vice-president has decided to stand up and be counted and to take responsibility for these new and unpopular procedures. On the other hand, he draws back into impersonality when he gets to the very negative material to avoid rubbing the purchasing managers' noses in the fact that their powers are being sharply reduced. But in the last paragraph the vice-president once again steps forward personally to state that all readers will "want to cooperate to the fullest."

Whether or not this final draft will be successful, we cannot know. What *is* important is that we have been able to manipulate our style and our organization—our way of saying things—to produce the tone we desire our reader to perceive. We have not written this memo thoughtlessly. We have simply engineered our writing to accomplish a particular task, in a given situation, with certain readers.

Of course, it doesn't matter whether you personally agree that this final version is what you would send in a real situation. What matters is that we have been able to think in intelligent terms about style, organization, and the tone our message produces.

You now have in your quiver not just one stylistic arrow, but several. And you now have the knowledge necessary to make intelligent choices of which arrow to use, in which situation, with which reader.

# 24

# HOW TO ANALYZE PROBLEM LETTERS AND DEVISE A WINNING RESPONSE STRATEGY

When someone writes to you or your company, you must respond to that letter. What is the wisest way to devise the best and most appropriate response? You should not just blindly follow the style and organizational strategy we have agreed upon in our experiments. You must also take into consideration the style and organization pattern of the communication you are responding to, and you must take note of your emotional feeling about that letter's tone.

Figure 24–1 is an analysis sheet for letters to be answered. It asks a series of questions that force you to infer as much as possible about:

1. The power of the author of that letter.
2. The author's emotional attitude.
3. The type of message your response will seem to be (in the eyes of the reader).

4. The organizational pattern best suited to that type of message to that individual reader.

5. The style that seems strategically best to achieve your purpose.

Let's use another case to help us learn how to use this analysis sheet.

### Case

The president of ABCD Products, Inc., sent a letter to all industrial customers announcing price increases of 6 percent on most lines of communication equipment and also announcing increases in maintenance charges ranging between 10 and 15 percent on various units. In addition, the letter announced price increases in all of ABCD services, including long-distance charges and hourly charges for emergency repairs to customer equipment.

The letter, signed by the president, was written in the forceful personal style appropriate to a chief executive writing to subordinates. Every negative point about price increases was hammered home in short, subject–verb–object, active-voice sentences. Moreover, a direct organizational pattern was used. The letter began and ended with a recital of bad news for the customer. No explanations were given for why prices had to be raised.

At the time of the letter, the national economy was weak, inflation was running high, and business had been urged by government to try to hold the line on prices.

You are the administrative assistant to the president of ABCD, and your immediate task is to write responses for the president's signature to some angry customer letters that have come in as a response to the announcement of price increases.

## RESPONSES FROM THREE IRRITATED READERS

We use the analysis sheet to analyze three irritated replies for the purpose of engineering exactly the type of response that seems most likely to produce the desired reaction in each of these concerned readers.

### Letter 1

The first letter was written by Emily P. Reyman, chief of administrative services of a large suburban hospital. Ms. Reyman's letter was addressed to the division president and was bumped down to you for your response.

Dear Sir:

I'm writing in vigorous rejection of your letter so smugly announcing price increases.

It seems all too apparent that once customers are stuck with your equipment, you regard this as open season to raise usage maintenance charges. You can get away with this because the customer would find it difficult, costly, and burdensome to unload your equipment under the present conditions.

I find it especially obnoxious that you have increased prices so sharply simply for using what we've bought from you. I see no possible justification. The communication lines are not new, so there can be no reason for you to incur increased costs that have to be passed on to customers. I notice that you have not increased significantly purchase prices on new equipment. I'm dead certain you haven't done this because of competition—and the fact that new purchasers wouldn't stand still for it as we old purchasers must.

I am frankly disgusted with this escalating price pattern set by your company. And I certainly intend to let all of my professional contacts in the Boston, Hartford, New York area know how ABCD conducts its business.

Sincerely,

Emily P. Reyman

Turn to the analysis sheet and begin to apply the questions to Reyman's letters. The letter is itself written in a forceful personal style, with some touches of color. Words like "open season, "get away with," "especially obnoxious," and "frankly disgusted" colorfully and effectively make their point.

The tone of the letter is thoroughly unpleasant and very angry. In fact, your first task is to restrain yourself from retaliating in kind, without stopping to consider what response is best.

## GETTING INSIDE THE READER'S MIND

Ask yourself what Reyman is really asking for in this letter. What does she really want? Does she really think that the company will roll its prices back? Or that it will give her a special deal? That's unlikely. Then what does Reyman really want? Well,

1. The letter to be answered is itself written in what style?

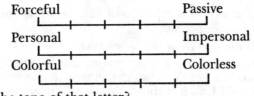

2. What is the tone of that letter?

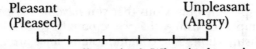

3. What is the writer really saying? What is the writer's purpose? What does the writer really want?

   Do you want to respond to the writer's real question/point, or is it best to ignore it or seem to miss the writer's point?

4. What are the facts in this situation? What is the most positive message possible in this situation?

5. What type of letter will you end up writing?

   Good news ☐       Negative persuasive ☐
   Bad news ☐        Positive persuasive ☐
   Informative ☐

6. What organizational pattern is usually best for that type of letter?

   Direct ☐                      Indirect ☐

7. What style usually best suits the type of message and organizational pattern you intend to use?

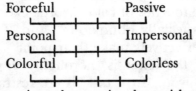

8. Does the style you intend to use involve a risk of augmenting too greatly the impact of the organizational pattern selected? Does the combination have too great a potential for causing the reader to react unfavorably to your tone?

   Yes ☐            No ☐

   If so, should you use (in all or part of your letter) a style and organizational pattern that blunt each other's impact on the reader?

   Yes ☐            No ☐

FIGURE 24–1. Analysis Sheet for Letters to Be Answered

she is obviously very angry and wants to yell at someone. You suspect that if you contradict her, you will only make her angrier. There is no substitute you can offer for the price increases that have been announced.

But now you begin to ask yourself what Reyman is actually upset about. She certainly cannot be too upset about the very minor increases that have been made in charges. It's possible that Reyman has been herself on the receiving end of many an angry letter occasioned by the escalation in health-care charges. Maybe she is actually enjoying having the shoe on the other foot for a change. Maybe all she really wants is some stroking and a dignified response from the president of ABCD. That is about all you can give her, so let's begin to think along those lines.

The facts of the matter are that maintenance prices on Reyman's equipment increased $23 per month—less than 8 percent—since the date of purchase in January a year ago. These prices were not affected by the current December announcement. Her hospital's long-distance charges will increase $8 a month, approximately 4 percent.

You have to produce a letter that is able to persuade Reyman to accept this negative information. One possibility is to write a negative persuasive message. But can you couch your message in such a way that you end up writing a positive persuasive letter? You would have to package what you have to say to persuade her that your price increases are, though seemingly negative, actually for the purpose of enabling you to maintain the high quality of services ABCD offers.

But you know that while you intend to make your message seem positive persuasive, she will surely regard it as negative. Therefore, even though you will try to be positive, it is important to use a circuitous pattern.

Now we have to determine the style that seems appropriate for this type of letter. To put it mildly, Reyman seems to be somewhat forceful by nature. If you use a style that responds too passively to her, she may be encouraged in her aggressive mood. On the other hand, if you use a very forceful style, you run the risk of sounding belligerent and argumentative. You have to remember that she is a customer; you are writing upward. But you are also writing a letter that has to be signed by ABCD's president, so it should not appear too weak and passive.

As a result of these thoughts, ask yourself whether you should use a style and organizational pattern that counteract each other.

You could mix, for example, a passive impersonal style with a direct organizational pattern. Or you could mix a forceful style with a circuitous organizational pattern. We know from our experiments that you should probably not be personal in style since this is a message that is negative in the reader's eye.

This, of course, is a judgment call. But let's suppose that you decide that it is unwise to allow the president of the division to be cast in too weak a posture. Therefore, you opt to do the following:

1. Since Reyman will consider the message to be negative, use a circuitous organizational pattern that will give you time to try to convince her that what she perceives as negative is actually positive.
2. But since you are arguing that these price increases are mandated by your desire to give her quality products and services in a time of escalating costs, you will present your arguments in a forceful style.
3. You will not, however, use a personal style. You will remain cool, calm, and collected, but somewhat impersonal.

Let's see what such a letter might look like:

Dear Ms. Reyman:

Thank you for sharing your concerns about the price increases just announced. Please be assured that this decision was made not to maximize profits but for the purpose of guaranteeing the very best of services.

As a member of the health-care profession, you are particularly aware of the escalating costs of the labor and materials that support your hospital's professional services. All too frequently, it is difficult, if not impossible, to make people realize that if one is dedicated to offering the best service, as does both our company and your profession, price increases become inescapable in times like these.

You will be reassured to know that the impact on your operation will be quite minimal. Our records show that the maintenance prices on your equipment have increased $23 per month—less than 8 percent—since your purchase in January of last year. And these prices were unaffected by the December announcement this year. Your long-distance charges will increase approximately $8 a month, about 4 percent, if your usage remains the same.

If my facts are correct, these increases compare most favorably with the varying national indicators of inflation and cost of living. However, I agree that no price increase is pleasant. Please accept my assurance that we will continue to make every effort to offset cost pressures through our own expense reduction programs before passing them along in the form of higher prices.

Sincerely,

Consider this draft and ask some questions. Does it make the president seem either too passive or too overbearing? No, the president forcefully takes responsibility for the price increases but argues that they were necessitated by ABCD's desire to offer quality goods and services. The president appears quite cool, calm, and businesslike. He does not sound either defensively apologetic or quarrelsomely offensive. The mixture of circuitous organization and forceful style has worked.

## Letter 2

The next letter we have to answer comes from Charles T. Warner, a Certified Public Accountant who sent this handwritten letter to the president of the division:

Dear Sir:

Our President is doing his best to decrease government spending and stop the inflationary price spiral. But he needs the help of responsible business leaders like you!

Your announcement concerning yet another round of price increases is in effect an attack on our national well-being. And ABCD is not alone. Other huge companies are also failing to live up to their public responsibilities.

Responsible restraint by business leadership is vital to saving our economy from ruin. It used to be unions and their greed that we businessmen complained about. Now the enemy is *ourselves!*

My office uses your products and finds them to be excellent. We hope to continue using them.

Be as much a leader yourself as your products are!

Sincerely,

## CHOOSING THE APPROPRIATE RESPONSE

Once again, turn to the analysis sheet to assist us in determining the organizational pattern and the style that your response should take.

First of all, we recognize that Warner's letter is indeed forceful and personal. Its tone is, oddly enough, pleasant. This is not an angry man libeling the company and making wild accusations. It is a person who really respects ABCD but is disappointed that ABCD has not done more to hold down prices in this time of economic unrest and spiraling inflation. The letter is like a lecture being given to the company by a caring uncle or former teacher.

What is Warner asking for? What does he really want? We get the feeling that he is a patriotic sort of person who is concerned more about the general inflationary spiral than about the particular impact upon his own operation. Therefore, we suspect that he does not want to enter into a discussion about how minimal the impact would be on his accounting firm. Instead, we guess that he expects a somewhat philosophical letter from the president of the company to reassure him that the company does indeed care about the economy and that prices are only increased as an absolute last resort.

The only thing Warner has actually asked for is that ABCD should be a "leader." Therefore, he is not trying to put the company down; rather, he is urging the company to accept its leadership role. So why not give him what he wants—a philosophical letter about the company?

The facts of the matter here are that while some prices have been raised as much as 15 percent, the majority of customers will not be affected to any substantial degree. Warner's own maintenance invoice will increase approximately 3 percent. This will bring his average annual increase to less than 10 percent.

Is there any way that you can make this type of letter positive? Our strategy has ruled out making the letter strictly informative, telling him how little his own firm will be affected by the price changes. This is not what Warner probably wants. He's a CPA who is quite capable of assessing the trivial effects of these price changes on his office. You can be positive if you write a letter that assures Warner that the company does care about the economy, does care about controlling inflation, and, in fact, cares about him, too.

We know that positive and positive persuasive messages probably should be more direct than circuitous in organizational pattern, more forceful than passive, and more personal than impersonal in style. Therefore, take as your goal writing a direct letter in a forceful, personal style.

Next, you must consider whether this style and organizational pattern have much potential for causing the reader to react unfavorably to your tone. Probably not. Warner does not seem to be howling for your scalp. A philosophical discussion by the president about the difficulties of keeping prices down in troubled times such as the present, spoken directly and personally to Warner, is probably exactly what Warner subconsciously hoped for.

Here is what such a letter might look like:

Dear Mr. Warner:

I want you to know that I very much appreciate your writing to me directly and expressing your concerns about the national economy and the inflationary spiral. I regret that the occasion was that we had to raise prices here at ABCD. And I want to assure you right off that we do everything possible to absorb cost increases internally before we even consider passing them along to valued customers like you.

An experienced businessperson such as yourself, however, knows that there comes a time when such cost increases cannot be absorbed without some action being taken. We have steadfastly refused to lower the quality of our products and our services, so that alternative is removed. And the alternative of holding the line on prices at the expense of negative effects upon our already quite low profit margin in effect passes on the negative impact to our stockholders.

While no price increases are pleasant, the price increases announced by ABCD actually compare most favorably with the varying national indicators of inflation and cost of living. But, despite this fact, in the attempt to offer the kind of responsible business leadership your letter calls for, we will continue, I assure you, to make every effort to offset cost pressures by our own expense reduction programs before passing costs along in the form of higher prices.

In conclusion, I am very gratified that you find our products to be more than satisfactory and, in turn, I wish to thank you for reminding me of the responsibility that ABCD has to fight in every way possible against the ills of inflation. I assure you that I will keep your message firmly in mind.

Sincerely,

How do you think Warner would react to this letter? He'd probably love it and show it to all his cronies at the country club. It answers Warner's letter frankly, forcefully, and, above all, respectfully. It doesn't make the president of the company whine or sound defensive. Therefore, the president will probably also be pleased.

## Letter 3

The next letter comes from A. B. Henry, the manager of a large golf club. Henry writes to the president of ABCD as follows:

Dear Sir:

I just received your new price list of increased charges. I'm at a loss to understand the justification for two price increases since October's billing.

[Mr. Henry then includes a paragraph of comparative price increases that indicate that on ABCD product A the maintenance costs have risen 26 percent, and on product B, 82 percent]

If we raised the price of golf like you do, soon everyone would be playing ping pong!

It would be nice to be able to pass this increased cost on, but unfortunately our members wouldn't like it any more than I do. Could you explain?

Sincerely,

Again, turn to your analysis sheet (Figure 24–1) and attempt to determine the kind of letter you should send to Henry.

We note that Henry's letter is written in a forceful and personal style, which seems to be the style used by customers when they are strongly objecting to something.

However, for the first time this customer's letter contains a colorful stylistic touch. The statement, "If we raised the price of golf like you do, soon everyone would be playing ping pong," is quite colorful and witty. We wonder whether we should give this sentence heavy weight in our analysis of the kind of style we should use when we respond to Henry. It's quite possible that the type of person who writes to us and evidences some wit and good nature deserves more than an impersonal textbook style of prose in the response he or she gets. But we know the dangers of being inappropriately colorful.

The tone of Henry's letter is not nasty or unpleasant. But while the tone of the letter is pleasant, it would be stretching things to assume that he was pleased to be informed about the price changes. However, we conclude that he is a reasonable person who deserves a reasonable answer.

Here are the facts of the matter. ABCD announced two maintenance price changes during the past year, approximately six months apart. The first, announced in June, was effective on October 1. The second, announced in December, will become effective on April 1 of the following year. The interval between the two changes is six months.

What is Henry really saying and what does he really want?

If his figures are correct, he has a valid point about being caught in a series of rapid maintenance price increases. It seems it would do you no good to ignore the fact that he has a valid point. Now regarding what Henry really wants, we doubt very much if he expects any general price increase to be applied to everybody but himself. There is little chance that he reasonably expects preferential treatment about his prices. What then does he want?

First of all, we suspect he wants an admission on the part of the company that what he reports has made its point—that he is right. We also think he wants—and deserves—an explanation of how and why these rapid-fire price increases took effect. You decide against arguing with him that these price increases took place over a six-month period instead of a two-month period as he implies.

Now you have to consider the type of message you are going to write. The only possible positive note you can think of is the fact that he is indeed right and that somehow the company is going to help him deal with the problem he has pointed out. You resolve to try to figure out something to offer him to perhaps make up for the difficult time ABCD has been giving his company.

Now consider what kind of organizational pattern is best for that type of letter. Recognize that if you can in any way turn your message even remotely into a positive letter, then you should use a direct pattern and a forceful and personal style. If, on the other hand, you cannot find anything positive to say or offer, then probably a circuitous, passive, impersonal approach might be better.

At this point, you decide to take a chance on writing a direct letter in a forceful, personal style—and even try to add a touch of color, out of respect for his "ping pong" witticism:

Dear Mr. Henry:

You are absolutely correct about the impact on your company of our two maintenance price increases during the past year. General costs of doing business have increased rapidly over the past two years. And the frequency of price increases has reflected those extraordinary cost pressures.

Let me assure you, however, that we consider price increases as a last alternative. We make every effort to offset cost pressures through our own cost expense reduction programs before passing them along to our customers in the form of higher prices. But we feel strongly that we have an obligation to continue to provide the highest quality service possible, even if that high quality of service must be supported by increased prices.

But that general fact does not solve your immediate problem. For that reason I am asking Albert Smith of our Savannah office to visit with you for the purpose of reviewing the equipment you have, with an eye to determining whether improvements in your costs can be effected. And it is quite possible that improvements are possible.

ABCD products A and B, which you own, are becoming increasingly difficult for us to maintain. Neither of these products is any longer being marketed by ABCD, and parts stocks are increasingly expensive to carry. In addition, the fixed costs of keeping our maintenance personnel properly trained on older-technology equipment must now be covered over a progressively smaller number of maintenance customers. These facts, to a great extent, explain the price increases you have experienced.

You will find Mr. Smith very helpful, I know. And I assure you, Mr. Henry, that I personally want to do everything possible to keep from being able to afford playing only ping pong.

Sincerely,

This draft begins on a note positive to Henry. There is always satisfaction in being told we are right!

Also, after justifying your price increases on the grounds of quality goods and services, you move quickly to offer Henry the services of Albert Smith. You explain that Henry's outmoded equipment may well be the cause of his troubles. But you do not spoil your letter by having the president try to make a sale. That would be inappropriate. Finally, you make a bow to Henry's witticism, just enough to let him know that he gave you a chuckle. That also might please him. But if you are at all unsure about the appropriateness of humor (and being colorful), out it should go!

# 25

## THE SUMMING UP

Early in this book, we said that style must be discussed sensibly in the work situation, but in order for people to do so, a common vocabulary had to be developed. Our sincere belief is that we have done the latter. Accomplishment of the former depends on you—how you use what we have learned to give guidance to those you supervise and counsel to those who supervise you.

"The Wheel of Style" should prove to be a useful tool for you and your colleagues to assess what style and what organizational pattern are probably best to use when conveying various types of messages. Together with this book, "The Wheel of Style" gives both boss and assistant a common vocabulary and a common approach to communications problems.

It is our hope that no longer will bosses wave their arms around and sputter, "I just don't like the way you said this. That's not my style!" Both boss and assistant will know that there is no such thing as one perfect style for all message situations and all readers. Both will know that proper style choice depends on the type of message being sent, the style that augments or counteracts the impact of the organizational pattern being used, and the style that is respectful of the relative positions of writer and reader. What we hope for is that in the business offices throughout the country, meaningful discussions of style strategy can now take place.

We recognize that there are built-in obstacles. Many subordinates have writing chores routed directly to them. As a result, there is often no chance for subordinates to discuss style strategy with the boss. In large companies, the signer of a memo may be two or three levels removed from the writer. And the draft may have to be approved by everyone in the line of command.

In such instances, rather than merely presenting a draft to the boss (or the bosses) for signature, the subordinate might well be wise to append a note, e.g., "This seems to be a very sensitive, negative situation. Therefore, I deliberately did not write in the usual forceful, general business style you prefer. Instead, I thought it wise to draw back into a largely impersonal and essentially passive style." As a result of a note like this, the boss will not jump to the conclusion that the assistant has written a dull, passive, low impact letter by accident.

Also, when superiors do personally route difficult writing situations to assistants, they could save much time (and mutual distress) if they told the subordinate what style seemed strategically wise to them as a result of their analysis of the situation and their personal relationship with the reader.

Figure 25–1 shows a form that might prove more useful and convenient than individually composed notes sent between boss and subordinate. This form serves to force a consensus of answers to these vital questions before the round robin begins:

1. What type of message are we sending?
2. What organizational pattern fits this type of message?
3. What style suits this message, its organizational pattern, and our relationship to the reader?

But what happens if, as is often the case, no one really has a clear sense of what style *is* best? We have seen, through the experimentations in this book, that we often have to draft a response in one style first, and if that doesn't sound quite right, alter the style appropriately one way or the other. Actually, in difficult communication situations, it is extremely unlikely that you are going to dash off a first draft that you or anyone else is going to sign. In fact, it is only the amateur who even expects writing perfection on the first try, except in the most routine of communications. In a very difficult situation, it might be a good idea to create more than one draft and either sleep on them yourself or let your boss decide which draft is best.

Naturally, there is no way that you, your boss, or "The Wheel of Style" can guarantee that any particular style strategy will prove effective with any given reader. "The Wheel of Style" deals in probabilities—but quite high probabilities. And at least you won't be communicating blindly or brainlessly.

You must recognize that "The Wheel of Style" only suggests; you will have to temper its advice by your own experience and knowledge of the situation and reader at hand. But no longer will you approach an important letter situation in doubt. With the help of "The Wheel of Style" you will approach it as scientifically as the inexact nature of human communication allows.

Check as appropriate.

Type of message: Positive ☐
Negative ☐
Information Conveying ☐
Negative Persuasive ☐
Positive Persuasive ☐

Written:
Up ☐
Down ☐

Type of organizational
pattern appropriate:  Direct ☐
Circuitous ☐

Style which is appropriate
to message, organizational
pattern and relationship
to reader:

| | | | | | |
|---|---|---|---|---|---|
| Forceful | ☐ | ☐ | ☐ | ☐ | Passive |
| Personal | ☐ | ☐ | ☐ | ☐ | Impersonal |
| Colorful | ☐ | ☐ | ☐ | ☐ | Colorless |

FIGURE 25–1. Style Strategy Form

FIGURE 25–2. The Wheel of Style

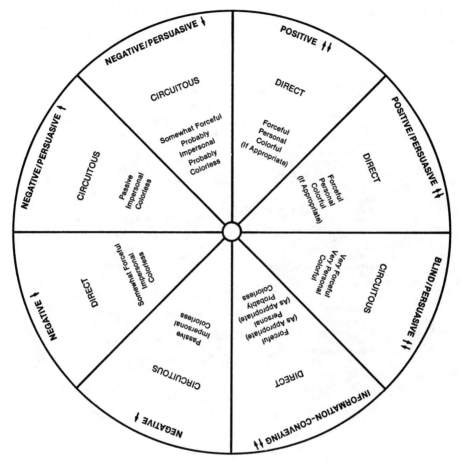

FIGURE 25–2. The Wheel of Style, cont'd.

**Forceful Style**

- Use active voice.
- Give orders—use the imperative!
- Do not beat around the bush; step up front and be counted.
- Use subject-verb-object sentences.
- Avoid "weasel" words like: "possibly," "maybe," "perhaps."

**Personal Style**

- Use active voice.
- Use persons' names, especially first names.
- Use personal pronouns, especially "you" and "I."
- Use the short sentences of ordinary conversation.
- Use contractions ("can't," "won't," etc.).
- Direct questions at the reader.

**Colorful Style**

- Use adjectives and adverbs.
- Use (if appropriate) metaphors, similes and other figures of speech.
- Be conversational or breezy.

**Passive Style**

- Avoid imperatives—never give an order!
- Use passive voice heavily.
- Attribute responsibility for negative statements to faceless, impersonal "others."
- Use "weasel words."
- Use long sentences and fat paragraphs.

**Impersonal Style**

- Avoid using persons' names, especially first names.
- Avoid using personal pronouns, especially "I" and "you."
- Use the passive voice.
- Avoid the brisk, direct, simple sentence style of conversation.

**Colorless Style**

- Avoid using adjectives, adverbs, metaphors, similes and other figures of speech.
- Blend impersonal style with passive style.
- Use formal words and expressions to freeze out any semblance of wit, liveliness, and vigor.

FIGURE 25–2. The Wheel of Style, cont'd.

# INDEX

# NOTES

# NOTES

# NOTES

# NOTES

# NOTES

# NOTES

# NOTES